Praying the Rosary for Spiritual Warfare

Fr. Dwight Longenecker

Our Sunday Visitor

www.osv.com
Our Sunday Visitor Publishing Division
Our Sunday Visitor, Inc.
Huntington, Indiana 46750

Our Sunday Visitor Publishing Division, Our Sunday Visitor, Inc., 200 Noll Plaza, Huntington, IN 46750; 1-800-348-2440

ISBN: 978-1-68192-021-4 (Inventory No. T1779)
eISBN: 978-1-68192-022-1
LCCN: 2016938902

Cover design: Amanda Falk
Cover art: © Starblue | Dreamstime.com
Interior design: Dianne Nelson

PRINTED IN THE UNITED STATES OF AMERICA

For Benedict, Madeleine, Theodore, and Elias

CONTENTS

IV. The Glorious Mysteries

INTRODUCTION

Are you disturbed and worried by the state of our world? When you hear of the atrocities committed by Islamic terrorists, witness the moral breakdown of society, and read about the disintegration of marriage, the gender wars, the increasing financial inequality and heartbreaking poverty, do you question what on earth is going on? When you see devastating tsunamis, earthquakes, floods, and violent storms, do you wonder if the world is about to crumble and fall?

When you hear about the frightening advance of biotechnology, global pollution, war, terrorism, torture, and genocide, do you feel as if the dark side is winning? When you read about abortion, child abuse, euthanasia, and the sale of baby body parts, do you feel helpless in the face of an overwhelming evil? When you see rising crime, irrational rage in society, and violence in the streets while corrupt politicians do nothing, do you fall into fear and confusion? Do you wonder what you can do to stem the tide? Do you feel as if Satan is a gigantic, ravenous, and relentless monster and that you are helpless? Do you wonder how you can do anything at all against such reckless hate?

The battle in our day is acute, and like many, I feel things will get worse before they get better. While the darkness seems ascendant, we must remember that the battle against evil has been going on from the beginning of time. The battle against evil is not just between "the dark side of the force" and those who want to stand for goodness, truth, and beauty. The battle is real, and it is personal.

The Ancient Serpent

The devil is not just a malignant "force" of the "dark side." He is a personal spiritual being. St. John calls him the great dragon or "that ancient serpent" (Rev 12:9), and St. Peter warns, "Be sober, be watchful. Your adversary the devil prowls around like a roaring lion, seeking some one to devour" (1 Pet 5:8). Jesus says about the devil, "He was a murderer from the beginning, and has nothing to do with the truth, because there is no truth in him. When he lies, he speaks according to his own nature, for he is a liar and the father of lies" (Jn 8:44).

The devil is not the opposite of God. He is a being created by God. As the *Catechism of the Catholic Church* explains:

> Scripture and the Church's Tradition see in this being a fallen angel, called "Satan" or the "devil." The Church teaches that Satan was at first a good angel, made by God: "The devil and the other demons were indeed created good by God, but they became evil by their own doing." (CCC 391)

It is very important, therefore, to realize that God did not create evil. He cannot create evil. God can create only what is good. To emphasize the original goodness of Satan, in the Old Testament he is referred to as the "Day Star" (Is 14:12), and Hebrew tradition teaches that he was the wisest and most beautiful of the angels.

Understanding Evil

Every warrior must understand his enemy. Understanding that Satan was originally the most beautiful of angels is vital for our understanding of evil itself. Satan's original goodness and his subsequent fall into pride and rebellion against God illustrate the fact that, although the consequences of evil are very real, evil has no positive reality in itself.

Consider darkness or cold. We perceive them as real, but darkness is nothing in itself. It is the absence of light. Likewise, although we shiver with cold, the cold is really only the absence of heat. Evil is similar. There is nothing positive or original about evil. Like cold and darkness, evil has no substance of itself. Evil is always either the absence of goodness, truth, and beauty, or it is a distortion and destruction of goodness, truth, and beauty.

Another way of saying this is: God creates, and what he creates is always good. Satan cannot create anything. All he can do is destroy and distort the good things God creates. As J. R. R. Tolkien has written about the evil one, "[He] can only mock, [he] cannot make." Evil is by its very nature destructive, violent, lying, distorting, twisting, and ugly. Jesus said it: "[Satan] was a murderer from the beginning" (Jn 8:44). Satan hates everything that is beautiful, good, and true, and he wants to kill it. Because he is the father of lies, he will lie and distort the truth wherever and whenever it occurs.

Seeing evil in this way gives us the foundation for battling against evil. In spiritual warfare, we will not so much wrestle with evil itself — that would be to wrestle with shadows in the dark. The way to counter the dark is to light a lamp. The way to battle cold is to start a fire. Therefore, instead of wrestling the shadows in the dark, we battle against evil best by supporting in prayer everything that is beautiful, good, and true.

Weapons and Warriors

The first thing Jesus did after his baptism was to go into the wilderness to do battle with the ancient foe. And like the Lord, we must make battling the enemy a priority.

Writing to the Christians at Ephesus, St. Paul gives a battle cry:

> Finally, be strong in the Lord and in the strength of his might. Put on the whole armor of God, that you may be able to stand against the wiles of the devil. For we are not contending against flesh and blood, but against the principalities, against the powers, against the world rulers of this present darkness, against the spiritual hosts of wickedness in the heavenly places. Therefore take the whole armor of God, that you may be able to withstand in the evil day, and having done all, to stand. Stand therefore, having fastened the belt of truth around your waist, and having put on the breastplate of righteousness, and having shod your feet with the equipment of the gospel of peace; besides all these, taking the shield of faith, with which you can quench all the flaming darts of the Evil One. And take the helmet of salvation, and the sword of the Spirit, which is the word of God. (Eph 6:10-17)

In their own way, each of the saints down the ages has affirmed that to be a Christian is to be a warrior. St. Benedict says that his monks are to be trained as "soldiers in the Lord's army," and the gentle St. Thérèse of Lisieux cries out with a militant voice, "Sanctity! It must be won at the point of a sword!" The list of saints who spoke about the need for spiritual warfare would take up most of this book. They all agree that not only are we engaged in a spiritual battle but also that prayer is the chief weapon and that the Mother of Jesus is the most important captain in the army.

St. Pio of Pietrelcina testified, "The strength of Satan, who is fighting me, is terrible, but God be praised, because He has put the problem ... into the hands of our heavenly Mother. Protected and guided by such a tender Mother, I will keep on fighting as long as God wishes." St. Louis de Montfort teaches, "The Hail Mary, the Rosary, is the prayer and the infallible touchstone by which I can tell those who are led by the Spirit of God from those who are deceived by the devil. I have known souls who seemed to soar like eagles to the heights by their sublime contemplation and yet were pitifully led astray by the devil. I only found out how wrong they were when I learned that they scorned the Hail Mary and the Rosary, which they considered as being far beneath them."

Mary, Trampler of Satan

The most compelling images of the Blessed Virgin Mary always show her with the child Jesus, while trampling a serpent underfoot. This is a direct reference to the prophecy in Genesis 3:15, in which God curses Satan, saying: "I will put enmity between you and the woman, and between your seed and her seed; he shall bruise your head, and you shall bruise his heel." The Fathers of the Church rightly referred to the Blessed Virgin as "the second Eve." Whereas the first Eve gave in to Satan, the second Eve defeated him. The ancient prophecy that she would crush his head is fulfilled as Jesus dies on the cross and the sorrowful Mother suffers with him. On the mountain of sacrifice, the offspring of the woman defeats Satan once and for all. Then in the twelfth chapter of Revelation, in dramatic dream language we see that Mary is engaged in battle with the "great red dragon" (12:3) and is not overcome.

Why is the Blessed Virgin Mary such a powerful warrior against Satan? Because he is overwhelmingly proud and she is the epitome of humility. Monsignor Léon Cristiani, in *Evidence for Satan in the Modern World*, writes:

The Devil fears the Virgin Mary more, not only than men and angels but, in a certain sense, than God himself. It is not that the wrath, the power and the hatred of God are not infinitely greater than those of the Blessed Virgin, since Mary's perfections are limited: it is because, in the first place, Satan, being proud, suffers infinitely more from being overcome and punished by the little, humble servant of God, her humility humiliating him more than the divine power; and secondly, because God has given Mary such great power over devils that, as they have often been obliged to admit, in spite of themselves, through the mouths of possessed persons, they are more afraid of one of her sighs of grief over some poor soul than of the prayers of the saints, and more daunted by a single threat from her than by all their other torments.

Mary is also powerful against Satan because she is the one created human being who has a unique relationship with God. God's Son took his flesh from the young girl from Nazareth. Through this supernatural transaction, and by the power of her son's redemptive death, Mary was filled with God's power in a completely unique and amazing way.

She was fully human, but the Son of God took her human flesh, and through her ultimate glorification in her assumption into heaven, she retains a unique role in the ongoing battle between the forces of heaven and the dark forces of this world.

From his long and bitter battles with Satan, St. Louis de Montfort encourages us by the power of the Rosary:

Even if you are on the brink of damnation, even if you have one foot in hell, even if you have sold your soul to the devil as sorcerers do who practice black magic, and even if you are a heretic as obstinate as a devil, sooner or later you will be converted and will amend your life and save your soul, if — and mark well what I say — if you say the Rosary devoutly every day until death for the purpose of knowing the truth and obtaining contrition and pardon for your sins.

Fighting Beside Our Mother

One of the great characters in the film trilogy *The Lord of the Rings* is Éowyn. She is the warrior princess of Rohan, and in her greatest scene she fights the Witch-King, one of the demonic Nazgûl. As the Witch-King prepares to strike Éowyn, he growls, "No man can kill me." Then Éowyn, sweeping off her helmet to reveal that she is a woman, retorts, "I am no man," and kills the Witch-King with her sword.

When I watch that scene, I envision the Blessed Virgin as a warrior like Éowyn. As we pray the Rosary, we are fighting beside our Mother Mary, who is a fearless, yet gentle, warrior. Her humility is triumphant, and her purity is powerful. Through the Rosary, we walk with her through each mystery of victory over Satan, and at every stage we battle with her against the ongoing evil.

Battling side by side with Mary is a joyful and victorious enterprise of prayer. God has done great things for her (Lk 1:49), and with her we can sing: "The LORD has done great things for us; we are glad" (Ps 126:3). As we shall see, fighting the good fight with Mary at our side is a positive action of praise and a powerful action of prayer. In this way, we light a lamp in the dark world and spark the fire of the Holy Spirit in the shivering gloom of Satan's realm.

Repetition and the Rosary

The strength of the Rosary prayer is the repetition. Repetitious prayer takes us more deeply into meditation, identification, and participation in the mystery of God's work in the world. However, the repetition of the prayers is sometimes counterproductive. We lose focus. We get distracted, and at worst the Rosary can become a dull routine and a tiresome chore.

Books like my *Praying the Rosary for Inner Healing* have helped many people focus their Rosary prayer on a particular intention. The popularity of that book helped me to understand the need for a similar book that would help people focus their Rosary prayer on the intention of battling against evil. To do so, we must be reminded again that prayer is always a positive action. We do not so much pray *against* evil as we pray *for* all that is beautiful, good, and true. Through prayer, we join our will with God's to support and promote all the good he is doing in the world to counter the distorted, dark, and twisted evil.

A good way to envision this prayer is to see Mary not only as a warrior but also as a busy, happy, and productive mother. As a mother, she is not only the source of new life, but she is also the kind of mother who jumps out of bed in the morning ready to nurture her children. She wants to prepare good food for them and make sure they are well clothed and happy. She wants to create a beautiful, safe, and abundantly happy home. She welcomes guests, and she works hard to create a warm and lovely atmosphere. She doesn't sit around being grumpy and gossipy about all that is wrong. She rolls up her sleeves and does what she can to make things good. She doesn't become gloomy, paranoid, and self-obsessed about what is bad. She is full of confidence, joy, and hope as she bustles about, doing good and sharing her abundant and creative life with others.

That's what our Rosary prayer for spiritual warfare should be like. We are Mary's fellow soldiers, donning our armor with a glint in our eye, a song in our heart, and a spring in our step. We should also see ourselves as Mary's children, helping with the chores to make that happy household. We wage this war and build this home in full confidence, knowing that her son has already won the war and that the present battles are the mopping-up operations against a foe who refuses to give up.

How to Use This Book

The twenty chapters that follow help us focus on different aspects of the battle against evil as they relate to each particular mystery. So, for example, the mystery of Our Lady's Visitation to Elizabeth takes place during the gestation of Jesus and John the Baptist in their mothers' wombs. Therefore, while praying that mystery of the Rosary, we focus on the crime of abortion. We don't simply pray against abortion. Instead, we pray positively for pro-life workers, gynecologists, expectant parents, and all those who work with women in crisis pregnancies. We also pray for abortion-clinic workers, for those wounded by the violence of abortion, and for legislators and legal workers striving to enact pro-life laws.

Each of the twenty chapters, therefore, aligns the battle against evil with one of the mysteries of the Rosary. As Pope St. John Paul II has written, the pattern of the Rosary is the pattern of life. To help focus our prayer, each chapter contains a Scriptural passage concerning that mystery, followed by a reflection that unlocks the connection between the Gospel mystery and the shadow side of evil to which it is related. To facilitate meditation, an example of the particular evil in our society is given, along with a "vision" of how that evil can be overcome through prayer and positive action.

There follows a list of ten positive things to pray for — one for each Hail Mary bead, and the chapter ends with a recommended prayer that follows the Fátima prayer at the end of each decade.

Praying the Rosary for Spiritual Warfare is designed as a practical prayer book for serious Catholics. It can be used as a prayer resource for both individuals and groups.

HOW TO PRAY THE ROSARY FOR SPIRITUAL WARFARE

The Rosary is a pattern of prayer that helps us meditate more deeply on the life of Christ. As his life was a constant battle against evil, so the mysteries of the Gospel connect with this battle, and through this prayer we hold hands with Jesus and Mary in the spiritual battle.

We pray the Rosary by holding the rosary and saying one prayer for each bead. The spaces between the beads become spaces for silence and meditation.

There are many different ways to pray the Rosary, and different customs and prayers have grown up in different cultures and for different individuals.

Some people kneel to pray the Rosary, but to pray the Spiritual Warfare Rosary I recommend sitting comfortably, perhaps with a candle burning before an icon or a crucifix.

At the back of this book, you will find the words for the prayers if you do not know them. Most people begin by holding the crucifix on the rosary and reciting the Apostles' Creed. This is followed by reciting the Lord's Prayer (Our Father), three Hail Marys, and a Glory Be on the beads that connect the crucifix to the main circlet of beads. When you get to the medal that joins these two groups of beads, I recommend that you stop and dedicate this Rosary to the spiritual battle.

St. Michael the Archangel is a great spiritual warrior against Satan, so this is a good place to insert the Prayer to St. Michael or to use this prayer:

By the power of this Rosary, I pray the Blessed Virgin Mary to intercede for me, my family, and the whole world. By these prayers, I invoke St. Michael and my guardian angel to fight with me against evil through the power of the suffering, death, and resurrection of the one Lord, Jesus Christ. Amen.

St. John Paul II recommended beginning each decade by announcing the mystery for that decade and, taking a moment, holding the chain before the decade of beads while visualizing the events of this particular mystery. In this book, you will find material to help you visualize each event and apply it to the spiritual battle.

You may feel that God is doing wonderful things as you pray through a particular mystery. Maybe you feel he is directing your mind toward other spiritual battles. If so, take your time. Allow the Holy Spirit to work through your life and your prayers to support all that stands against evil. You may feel that you want to repeat that mystery. That's good. You may feel that you want to stop and simply rest in God's light and peace and not complete the entire sequence of mysteries. That's fine. Be led by the Spirit, and allow him to guide your prayer.

You may feel that the meditations designed for spiritual warfare don't apply to your situation. In that case, please continue to pray the Rosary to battle evil, but allow your prayers to be used by God for other people. Please pray also for those unknown to you, that they might triumph over evil, darkness, fear, and hatred.

Many people have doubts, questions, and fears about spiritual warfare. It's best not to worry too much about the details, but to be faithful. God knows what he is doing, and he will use our prayers as part of his great work in the world, even if we are not aware of how our prayers are changing things.

Have faith as you pray. Prayer is always answered. Something always happens! It's just that it is not for us to say what God will do.

If we pray faithfully, he will be faithful in keeping his promises. How and when he keeps his promises is his business! All we have to do is watch and wait, and eventually we will see the power of his victory over evil in our world.

I.

The Joyful Mysteries

Annunciation

Sexual Immorality

(Luke 1:26-38)

A beautiful girl is overshadowed by the Holy Spirit and says a simple yes. At that moment, the God-man is conceived. This ecstatic, life-starting encounter between the Blessed Virgin Mary and the Holy Spirit reflects the first moment of conception for each human being. Through the act of loving union between a man and a woman, a child is conceived. Through this tender and beautiful union, within the bonds of sacramental marriage, a husband and wife cooperate with God in the creation of new life. This joyful, loving act of creation is one of the most precious and pure gifts that God has given the human race.

The Dark Distortion

From the very beginning, in the Garden of Eden, Satan saw the love between a husband and his wife, and he hated it. He wanted to destroy it. Attacking the simple, joyful, and pure love between a husband and wife is still one of Satan's favorite crimes. God designed man and woman to share life and love, but Satan destroys that gift through the traps of sexual immorality and lust.

The list of sexual sins is a long one: sexual relations outside marriage, cohabitation, adultery, pornography, masturbation, prostitution, promiscuity, sodomy, and all kinds of selfish impurity. These things are evil not because the Catholic Church has decided arbitrarily that they are bad. The sins of sexual immorality are evil because they distort and destroy the beautiful, life-giving act of marriage.

The sexual act is designed, by its very nature, to be the intimate sharing of one's total self with a spouse. This is the human expression of divine love that each one of us longs for, but we are always looking for a shortcut. We want instant pleasure rather than the long-term, long-lasting delight of marriage. Sexual sins distort what should be an act of faithful self-giving into an action of selfish pleasure. A loving, faithful marriage is one of the best opportunities any man or woman has of achieving happiness in this life. But Satan hates the idea that we might be happy, and so he works long and hard to destroy one of God's most wonderful ways for us to have a happy and abundant life.

Witnesses from the Battle

Michael was a good-looking man in his twenties. He came to talk about his inability to find a good woman to marry. His relationships were short-lived, and while part of him wanted to marry, another part of him couldn't be bothered to take the trouble. A shadow side kept blaming the women he was dating for the repeated false starts and breakups.

Michael soon told me about his pornography problem and his life of casual sexual encounters, which worked against his desire to find a good marriage partner. Satan can get a strong hold over a person through their addiction to sexual sins. The sin makes them confused about love and sex. When many people in a population are consumed with sex addiction, the whole society becomes selfish, sick, and sterile.

Through pornography and promiscuity, a man or a woman substitutes a fantasy world and fleeting sexual encounters for a real relationship. The fantasy world of sex and short-term flings ends up leaving them feeling empty, guilty, and unsatisfied. They want a permanent love, but they are unable to make a real, pure, and lasting relationship. Their distorted and destructive sexual behavior paralyzes their ability to have a healthy relationship that might lead to marriage.

Michael decided to clean up his act. Part of his therapy was to pray the Rosary every day — focusing on the Joyful Mysteries. Because the Joyful Mysteries focus on the family life of Jesus, the Holy Spirit can make deep connections to heal our broken and distorted sexuality. By understanding the great goodness of God's gift of sexual love, Michael was able to move beyond his distorted life of lust and eventually begin a relationship that was solid and pure and moving toward marriage.

Meditate for Victory

As we meditate on the perfect conception of Jesus at the Annunciation, we can see the total purity and joy of the Blessed Virgin Mary. She is a beautiful young girl, as natural and delightful as a day in May. She receives the gift of a child in a moment of ecstasy and self-giving. This is the pure and abundant gift that God gives the human race as we share in his love, life, and light.

Imagine this innocence, abundance, and joy as a powerful force in the world. This is the purity and power of Mary — still active through the redeeming work of her son. Imagine this powerful purity radiating out into the world as an action of love and creativity. This is the beauty and power of a marriage between a man and a woman immersed in, and surging with, the sacramental love of God.

Now you can see how dark, distorted, and destructive sexual immorality is. Sexual sins are shallow, selfish, mean, and hopeless compared with the purity, goodness, and joy of a happy and faithful marriage. Imagine this goodness and power surrounding and supporting those who work to enhance and promote chastity and marriage. Use these battle points to focus your prayers.

Battle Points

On each bead, pray to support one of these good intentions:

- For those who teach chastity programs
- For those who teach "Theology of the Body"
- For counselors who help people with sexual addictions
- For priests who counsel those who confess sexual sins
- For those who struggle to live chastely
- For the single and celibate
- For those who are trapped in an unhealthy or sinful relationship
- For ministries that battle pornography
- For ministries that deliver men and women in the pornography industry
- For those who rescue men and women from prostitution and sexual abuse

After the Fátima Prayer

Heavenly Father, pour out your divine love on our
poor, broken human race. Give us the vision of your
purity and power. Banish the darkness of immorality
by the light of your everlasting love. Fill our hearts
with that chaste love so that we will not seek it in
distorted and destructive ways. This we pray through
the King of love, our Lord Jesus Christ. Amen.

Visitation

Abortion

(Luke 1:39-56)

*Two women, pregnant and full of joy, visit with each other.
The girl and her older cousin rejoice in the miraculous gift of
life. As they share their stories, the children in their wombs
recognize each other. One child leaps for joy. Both women
laugh with delight and sing God's praise. Both women are
secure in their faith and hope in God. The young woman is
especially blessed. She is completely full of God's grace, and
she nurtures her son with a totality of love and perfection.
As he grows in her womb, he knows absolute love, uncon-
ditional acceptance, and the fullness of God's grace present
in his mother's life. The older woman, yearning for a child
for so long, is filled with a quiet, overwhelming joy that at
last she is the bearer of new life.*

The Dark Distortion

The sexual act is, by its very nature, linked with the conception of a child. Artificial contraception separates the
sexual act from both the fact and the idea of a new human life,
so all that remains is the pleasure of sexual union. If a man and
a woman wish to eliminate children from the sexual act, then
those who wish to separate the sexual act from procreation will

eventually attempt to eliminate the children who are conceived but unwanted. Satan hates children and loves abortion.

In the crime of abortion, whether by abortifacient drugs or surgical procedure, the secure, nurturing environment of an unborn child is invaded. The innocent baby is killed and then flushed or torn from his mother's womb. In early abortions, the developing child is scraped from the womb or the child is dislodged and eliminated with chemicals. In later abortions, the child is poisoned and dismembered — and sometimes beheaded. In partial-birth abortions, the baby is delivered feet-first, then a scissors or other instrument punctures the base of his skull, whereupon a catheter is inserted and the brain is removed by a suction machine; this results in the collapse of the skull, and the abortionist then completes the delivery of the dead child.

For as long as human beings can remember, a child was considered to be a blessing, a joy, a new gift of life, and the hope for the future. When societies drifted into decadence and decay, the child was considered to be a burden and a curse. In our pleasure-crazed world, a pregnancy is too often greeted with dismay, and the parents destroy their own child. An unborn child is not only a new life but also a sign of how one can enter into union with God, for the Gospel says unless we become like little children we cannot enter Christ's kingdom. This is why Satan hates children and mothers and loves to destroy them through the horrible crime of abortion.

Witnesses from the Battle

Jenny knocked on my door one afternoon. I had never met her before but was shocked to see a young woman in her twenties doubled over in pain. I invited her in, and she began to explain that she was experiencing excruciating pains in her abdomen. The doctors could do nothing for her and were mystified. Painkillers didn't touch her constant agony.

Knowing that people often talk about their illnesses in symbolic ways, I asked her what the pain felt like. She said, "It feels like someone is tearing my insides out." Immediately, I suspected that she was experiencing post-abortion trauma. I asked her gently about her relationships, and the whole sad story of her affair with a married man, the pregnancy, and the forced abortion tumbled out.

Jenny's young life was wrecked by abortion, but together, with some prayerful people in the parish, we held a healing Mass in which Jenny forgave the man who forced the abortion on her. She asked forgiveness for her own part in the affair, and she named her unborn child and committed him to God. I showed her how to pray the Rosary for inner healing and explained how the mystery of the Visitation was especially helpful in healing her problem.

The next week Jenny came to see me, and I hardly recognized her. She stood pretty, proud, and tall. Her pain was completely gone, and she brought her best friend with her, saying, "I think Tracey needs to talk to you too…."

Meditate for Victory

Before you recite this decade of the Rosary, meditate on the mystery of the Visitation of Mary to Elizabeth. See the two pregnant women, and see their quiet but intense joy. Try to see in their faces the radiant glow so often evident when women are going to have a baby. See their quiet confidence and supreme delight in being part of God's plan of creation, and in sharing in their own bodies the mystery of new life.

Focus on the Blessed Virgin. She bears the gift of new life while also still bearing in her young body and soul the gift of complete purity and goodness by God's grace. This total goodness and purity is powerful in the world. The life she shares with her child is the life that brings light to the world. The life she shares with her child is the source of everlasting joy and life. Her womb is a foreshadowing of the tomb. As Christ will burst forth from her at Christmas, so he will eventually burst forth from the tomb at Easter. He is life itself. By him, all things live and move and have their being.

Every pregnant woman, to a lesser degree, shares in this marvelous mystery of life, so now we can see how horrible, tragic, and terrifying the crime of abortion really is. Not only does it pluck out the life of an unborn child, but it is also an attack on the very principle of the divine life itself. Abortion is a horror from hell. Abortion is violence. Abortion is death.

Battle Points

On each bead, pray to support one of these good intentions:

- For expectant mothers
- For women in crisis pregnancies
- For the fathers of unwanted, unborn children
- For pro-life campaigners
- For pro-life lobbyists and legislators
- For pregnancy counselors
- For gynecologists and women's medical staff
- For parents who have chosen life for a disabled child
- For adoption-agency workers
- For adoptive and fostering parents

After the Fátima Prayer

Heavenly Father, the source of all life and love, pour
down upon our angry and murderous world your
gift of joyful life. Deliver us from Satan's lie that a
new life is a burden and a curse. Strengthen all those
who work to eliminate the crime of abortion, and
strengthen and encourage all those who
have sacrificed to accept and nurture the gift of life.
Amen.

Nativity
Artificial Birth
(Luke 2:1-20)

Mary received God's word, conceived her son, and has carried him in perfect simplicity and natural goodness. Joseph has accompanied her every step of the way, and now the child is about to be born. Some ancient texts suggest that a local midwife comes to help with the birth, and that the miraculous birth of Jesus Christ is without the usual pains. The Gospel doesn't tell us this, but if Mary was, by God's grace, kept from original sin, then she would have been spared the pain of childbirth, which is part of the curse of sin. If this is so, can you see the pure delight at this birth in the stable that night? Can you share the wonder and joy in the eyes of Mary and Joseph and the birth of this perfect infant? In Jesus' conception, gestation, and birth, the natural is filled with grace from within so that all that is simple and natural is infused with supernatural goodness, purity, and beauty.

The Dark Distortion

The conception, gestation, and birth of a child are natural acts in which the husband and wife cooperate with God in the creation of a new human being. The natural goodness of this act is now being distorted and destroyed through a range of artificial technologies. We have taken control of procreation and are now able to turn the "baby machine" off and on at will.

Not only do we have artificial contraception, but we also have artificial conception. Men and women have sexual intercourse and block new life, while others spend huge amounts of money to have a child outside the boundaries of normal marriage and sexual intercourse.

Artificial insemination means a man's sperm (acquired by masturbation) is inserted into the woman with technology, not love. In vitro fertilization allows a woman's eggs to be fertilized by a man's sperm in the test tube and then implanted into a womb. Sperm and egg donation means the genetic material may be that of any man or woman, while surrogacy means the woman carrying the fertilized egg could be an anonymous female. The natural unity between husband, wife, and child has been ruptured. Sperm and eggs become products, so the child becomes a product — available for the person who has the money to pay for it.

Sperm donation, artificial insemination, in vitro fertilization, and surrogacy means homosexual couples can have children through the manipulation of technology. Gender reassignment surgery has even produced women who have "transitioned" to become men while retaining their womb so that the "father" gives birth. In the meantime, some men have "transitioned" to become women but retained their genitals to make sure they can still inseminate their lesbian partner. The entire natural order has thus been distorted and destroyed beyond the wildest imaginings of our parents and grandparents.

In addition to these horrors, medical technicians continue to experiment with genetic manipulation, human cloning, and "transhumanism" (through which traits of animals are genetically implanted into the human genetic code).

Witnesses from the Battle

An old college friend named Charlie spoke to me about the difficulties his family has gone through. He and his wife, Nancy, have four children. They weren't perfect parents, but they did their best to bring the children up with Christian values and principles. When Karen, their oldest daughter, came home from college and announced that she was a lesbian, Charlie and Nancy were disappointed.

Then Karen said she and her partner Chris were going to be married, and that Chris was not only pregnant through artificial insemination but that Charlie and Nancy's seventeen-year-old son was the sperm donor.

Meanwhile, their older son David said he was transgender and began to dress in women's clothing. Eventually, he moved in with his boyfriend, and Chris agreed to act as surrogate mother for a child produced with Karen's donated egg and David's boyfriend's sperm. Their young daughter cohabited with her boyfriend and eventually became pregnant outside of marriage.

Charlie and Nancy were hugely conflicted. Their Catholic faith called them to love and accept their children unconditionally, but they also could not accept their children's life choices. They still struggle daily to know how to love and accept not only their children but also their children's partners and their unusually produced grandchildren. They are doing their best, but the fact of the matter is that their family has been broken into pieces by the distortion and destruction of natural conception and birth, and they don't know how to put things back together.

Meditate for Victory

Stop for a moment and visualize the birth of Jesus and ponder the beauty of this natural-supernatural event. The birth of

Christ reveals to the world the beautiful and simple way God works. Although Jesus' conception and birth were completely unique, they reveal a startling insight into how God works in the world. He creates new life through the loving union of two people.

Within that loving embrace, the sperm and egg meet. The moment of conception is not merely a biological event. The conception of the child is bathed in the light of love, and in a sacramental marriage it is bathed in the blessing of God's love. The child's nine months of gestation and finally the child's birth are surrounded by prayer, goodness, love, and light.

It must be different for a child conceived in a test tube, implanted in the womb through technology, and carried in the womb of someone other than his mother. It must be different for a child who finds himself with two "mothers" or two "fathers." This is why children from these distorted relationships need love and acceptance, perhaps even more than a child conceived, carried, and born in natural conditions and circumstances.

Battle Points

On each bead, pray to support one of these good intentions:

- For childless couples
- For those who counsel childless couples
- For those who help childless couples achieve natural fertility
- For those who teach Natural Family Planning
- For those who counsel people with same-sex attraction

- For women driven through poverty to be surrogates
- For wisdom for those who work in the area of reproductive technology
- For wisdom for families of artificially produced children
- For children who were produced artificially
- For wisdom for those who work in the area of genetic engineering

After the Fátima Prayer

Father in heaven, you have chosen to cooperate
with husbands and wives in the creation of new
life through the sacrament of marriage. Help us to
understand those whose identities are distorted and
confused. Enable us to see clearly the beauty, truth,
and goodness of your plan for marriage, and give
us the strength to build strong, faithful, and joyful
families. Amen.

Presentation in the Temple
Child Abuse
(Luke 2:22-39)

It was the Jewish law that a sacrifice of thanksgiving would be offered at the birth of the first child. So a short time after his birth, Joseph and Mary take Jesus to be presented in the Temple. The young mother is full of simple joy and pride as she goes with her husband to make the sacrifice. There they meet two grandparent figures, Simeon and Anna. The four of them — the mother and foster father, and the old man and woman — welcome the child into the family of God, and through the ritual offering the boy's childhood begins with God's perfect blessing and a family full of acceptance and love. The presentation of Christ stands for the human stage of infancy and childhood, and his presentation in the Temple indicates that the childhood of Jesus was surrounded and filled with God's blessing and presence.

The Dark Distortion

The perfect childhood takes place within a secure, stable, and loving home, with a mother, father, and extended family. Parents, grandparents, relatives, and siblings surround the child with peace, love, security, and acceptance. This provides the perfect foundation for the child to grow into adulthood with confidence, creativity, and strength.

Satan hates children. He wants to destroy them, and so he destroys their happy home. Because of promiscuity, divorce, abandonment, and poverty, children are born and raised in broken homes with only one parent, stepparents, or foster parents. Children are abandoned and left in orphanages or even on the streets.

Neglected and abandoned children fall prey to physical abuse, violence, sexual abuse, pornography, child slavery, and prostitution. Sadly, the very ones they should be able to trust too often betray them. Teachers, pastors, neighbors, and friends rob the children of their innocence through sexual, emotional, spiritual, and psychological abuse. Some children even end up being tortured, raped, and killed.

Satan takes childhood — which should be a carefree time of innocence, security, happiness, and peace — and twists it into a time of heartache, stress, loneliness, terror, bitterness, and violence. Some of us take the little ones Jesus gathered into his arms and dash them against the rocks of our own lust, greed, and selfishness. If we treat children as disposable commodities and cause "these little ones ... to sin," it would be better if a millstone were hung around our neck and we were cast into the sea (Mk 9:42).

Witnesses from the Battle

Mack was a burly ex-soldier, but he was scared of becoming a father. A successful man with his own business, a kind and loving wife, and good friendships, he told me he was terrified of fatherhood because of his own childhood.

During counseling, he recounted how his drunken father would beat him and his sister with anything that was at hand. After the abusive father abandoned them, Mack's mother took up with another man who piled verbal and emotional abuse onto the two children — finally making them live in a shed, where, at the age of twelve, Mack had to fend for himself and his little sister. When the first stepfather disappeared, things got worse, and both children were sexually abused by the next man in their mother's life.

No wonder Mack was terrified of becoming a father. The only fathers he ever knew were monsters. Praying the Rosary for inner healing, along with a deep way of praying the Our Father, brought Mack the deep healing he needed. He had no models for positive fathering, but it was through the love, acceptance, and prayers of his pastor, men in his parish, and his mature and kindly father-in-law that Mack was able to find the way forward, not only into being a good dad but also into a mature and trusting relationship with God, his heavenly Father.

Meditate for Victory

Jesus grew up in Nazareth not only with the love of a perfect mother and foster father but also with the friendship, support, and care of Joseph and Mary's extended family. That Jewish extended family in the village of Nazareth probably included the children of Joseph's first marriage as well as aunts, uncles, and cousins. These are the kinsmen the Gospels record as Jesus' brothers and sisters.

Stop and visualize the happy tribe Jesus would have grown up with. His childhood was confident, innocent, and free. He was surrounded by cousins and half brothers and sisters. He was supported by noble, loving father figures and gentle, beautiful, and strong women. The Gospel says he "increased in wisdom and in stature, and in favor with God and man" (Lk 2:52). This is the picture of a perfect childhood, and this is the positive and joyful image we embrace as we meditate on this mystery.

How different it is for children whose lives are distorted and destroyed by poverty, promiscuity, broken homes, divorce, slavery, and all forms of abuse. As we pray the Rosary, we envision Jesus' perfect and carefree childhood, and we pray for God's supernatural strength and help for children whose lives are broken by abuse, and for all those who nurture and protect the precious gift of children.

Battle Points

On each bead, pray to support one of these good intentions:

- For parents and grandparents
- For brothers and sisters
- For those who struggle as single parents
- For teachers
- For children's doctors, nurses, and counselors
- For child-protection professionals
- For law-enforcement officials who battle child abuse
- For orphans and those who care for them
- For victims of child abuse to receive healing
- For guardian angels to watch over and protect our children

After the Fátima Prayer

Father in heaven, your Son entered our world as a little child. Watch over all children. Deliver us from those evils that cause the distortion and destruction of childhood. Help us to provide safe, loving, strong, and joyful communities where our children can be nurtured in confidence, educated with love, and formed in the image of the child Jesus Christ. Amen.

Finding in the Temple
Teen Tragedies
(Luke 2:42-52)

When a child is lost everyone panics. The child becomes distressed, and the parents become increasingly frantic looking for the child. When he is found, all is forgiven in the joy of the reunion.

The young mother and her husband look everywhere for their son, only to find him seated in the Temple precincts discussing theology and Scripture with the teachers and wise men. At the age of twelve, Jesus passes from boyhood into adolescence, and he answers his parents with respectful confidence, "Did you not know that I must be in my Father's house?" (Lk 2:49). Brimming with confidence and enthusiasm for his calling, at the age of twelve, Jesus is already taking the first steps on the adventure into adulthood.

The Dark Distortion

The teenage years are a time of adventure. The confident adolescent should use his secure and happy home as a launch pad into adult life. As the child's body changes, his mind and emotions also go through an upheaval. Like the boy Jesus in the Gospel story, the happy teenager grapples with intellectual challenges, learns how to be independent from his parents, and increasingly enjoys interaction with the outside world.

Satan hates the beauty and innocence of youth. In our dangerous and corrupt world, Satan twists the teenage years into a nightmare of rebellion, confusion, anger, and fear. Instead of launching out positively, teenagers rebel against all authority and drift into a distorted and destructive form of adolescence. Wandering alone in the world — refugees from their broken homes and dysfunctional families — they are gathered up by those who would offer them the false security and artificial families of gangs and negative peer groups.

Desperate for love, like the prodigal son, they seek affirmation and acceptance with the crowd, and bowing to peer pressure they slip into substance abuse, promiscuity, addiction, and crime. Vulnerable to older people who would betray their trust and exploit them, they become victims of sexual, physical, and emotional abuse. With no one to guide them, they make disastrous decisions, ending up in the hospital, the prison, or the morgue.

Satan hates the innocent, funny, and trusting beauty of teenagers. He wants to destroy them and shipwreck their lives before they even have a chance.

Witnesses from the Battle

I met Kevin when I was doing some rehabilitation work in a British prison. In a group, we listened to each man's story. Kevin was honest about his career in crime. Driven by a drug addiction, he began burglarizing houses to feed his habit at the age of thirteen.

By sixteen, he had already had a spell in prison, and on his second conviction, after a burglary that turned violent, he was given a ten-year sentence. Before he was scheduled to be released, I asked Kevin what he really wanted after he was a free man again.

"I just want to spend time with my daughter," he said.
I asked how old his daughter was.
"Fifteen," Kevin answered.
I paused. Kevin couldn't have been more than thirty himself. Then it dawned on me. Between his first jail sentence and the second, he'd fathered a child at the age of fifteen.

It's easy to see Kevin as just another criminal, and he admitted to his crimes, but in many ways Kevin was also the victim. Coming from a broken home, where he had been physically and sexually abused, he was entering adulthood already broken, distorted, and destroyed. A life that could have been promising, positive, and productive took an early downturn. If he had only had a foundation of love, faith, and hope, his life could have been so different.

Meditate for Victory

Can you use your imagination to see Jesus as a teenager? He must have been handsome, smart, and funny. He must have been full of energy, enthusiasm, and joy. No doubt the girls were giving him some glances, while the other boys gathered around the leadership of his natural intelligence, wit, and deep spirituality.

There are few things more joyful to experience than the beauty, energy, and drive of young people. Their laughter, edginess, and ability to think outside the box is refreshing and stimulating. Jesus brought all this to adolescence and more. Already he was aware of the intimate relationship he had with his heavenly Father. Already he was willing to share the truth, beauty, and goodness he understood with others.

Teenagers who drift into low self-esteem, rebellion, and insecurity show how Satan wants to destroy and distort the positive and joyful years of adolescence. As we pray the Rosary, we envision Jesus' perfect teenage years and ask for God's supernatural strength and help for all those who nurture, teach, protect, and form the precious gift of young people.

Battle Points

On each bead, pray to support one of these good intentions:

- For parents and grandparents of teenagers
- For middle school, high school, and college teachers
- For youth workers
- For coaches and mentors
- For those who counsel teenagers with problems
- For those who are disobedient to parents
- For young people struggling with addiction
- For the gift of chastity
- For those who work with young offenders
- For teenage victims of abuse

After the Fátima Prayer

Heavenly Father, watch over our teenagers and young
people. Deliver them from evil. Help them to know
the joy of their youth. Keep them safe from all harm
and help us to give them the love, acceptance, and
care they need as they launch out into life. Finally,
in your mercy, grant them the gift of confident faith,
that they might hear the call of Christ and follow
him with joy. Amen.

II.

The Luminous Mysteries

Baptism of the Lord

Antichrists and False Religions

(Matthew 3:16-17)

The Jews are at a fever pitch. All the ancient prophecies pointing to the coming of God's anointed One — the Messiah — have been fulfilled. Who will it be? From where will he appear? What will he be like? Will he come as a king and overthrow the Roman overlords? John the Baptist is a likely candidate. The crowds go to hear him and listen to his preaching and to be baptized. Suddenly the preacher stops. A young man steps from the crowd and moves forward to be baptized. The people are speechless. Somehow this man moves and behaves with total confidence, authority, and simplicity. In the midst of their confusion, weakness, and fear, this man moves with clarity of purpose, strength, and courage. They hear how this new preacher recently read from the Scriptures in his local synagogue with a startling claim to be the anointed One from God. He is a man with a mission, a man to be listened to, a man who will transform lives and transform the world.

The Dark Distortion

One of the main tasks of Jesus was to preach the truth. He not only taught the truth; he *was* the truth, the way, and the life. When he appears as the Christ — the anointed One — he incarnates God's word of truth in the world. This is why

St. John teaches, "The Word became flesh and dwelt among us, full of grace and truth" (Jn 1:14).

Satan hates the radiant simplicity of Jesus' life and teaching. That is why, from the earliest days of the Church, Satan has inspired Antichrists and false teachers. In the Acts of the Apostles, a magician called Simon drew people into the occult, and in St. Paul's epistles it is clear that there were false teachers who gathered people together, saying whatever they thought would please them (2 Tim 4:3-4). They did so not to serve the Lord but out of ambition, jealousy, and for personal gain (Phil 1:15-17). In the second chapter of the second letter of Peter, false prophets are predicted. They will bring heresies and blasphemies, and they will mislead many. Peter blasts them as wicked, greedy, self-absorbed unstable beasts.

The dark distortion of Jesus' ministry as the anointed teacher of the truth is Satan's constant and never-ending parade of false teachers, heresies, schismatic sects, pagan religions, false prophets, and artificial churches.

The false teachers are wolves in sheep's clothing (Mt 7:15). They smile and appear charming. They are smooth and artful teachers, but like their father, the devil, they are liars, and they hate the truth. The way you can tell a false teacher is to listen carefully to his or her attitude toward the Catholic faith. There are thousands of false prophets, untrue teachers, counterfeit churches, and false religions, but they all have one thing in common: they despise the authority of the successor of Peter, and they hate the Blessed Virgin, Jesus Christ's Catholic Church, and her sacraments.

Witnesses from the Battle

When I am at a speaking engagement and open up for questions, I can almost predict what the question will be as an older person raises his or her hand.

"Father, what can we do to help our children return to the Catholic faith?"

Their hearts are broken because their children and grandchildren have left the Church and joined another denomination, a Protestant sect, or left Christianity altogether for a strange cult, Eastern religion, or New Age philosophy. Some have simply stopped believing completely, swallowing the lie of atheism and relativism so prevalent in colleges and universities.

What can be done to combat false teaching and win our children back to the faith?

First, Catholics in authority need to stop teaching indifferentism and universalism. These are the lies that every religion is as good as any other, and that everyone will be saved in the end. No wonder people go church shopping if the priests and sisters themselves have told them that every other religion is just as good as Catholicism.

Next we need to know our faith. There are excellent resources available. We need to be able to give an answer to the faith that lies within us (1 Pet 3:15). Most of all, it is a good, consistent, and loving example combined with prayer — commending them to God, knowing that he will continue his work in their hearts, even if they stray from the fullness of the truth.

In ministry, I have seen time and again how Catholic young people take time out. They explore other religions and philosophies. Often the false teachers do great and permanent harm, but through a patient, loving, and sure witness the lost sheep find their way home.

Meditate for Victory

As you meditate on this mystery, think why we call these the *Luminous* Mysteries. It is because Jesus is the Light of the world, and everything he does in his ministry and in his being is filled with a wonderful radiance.

Therefore, see Jesus coming up out of the waters of baptism like the sun dawning after a dark night. The heavens open. The clouds part, and a beam of light shines on him from above. He exudes pure joy and the bright radiance of heaven itself. This light of the world also shines through all of his teachings and the teachings of his Catholic Church.

False teachers mix shadow with this light. They corrupt the truth with their falsehoods. False prophets and counterfeit religions are noted for their shiny, seductive outward appearance, but underneath they are full of darkness and deceit. Christ's light-filled teaching banishes the false prophets and counterfeit religions not through teaching and theory alone but by being lived out day by day in the lives of the saints, and through the fullness of truth in his Church.

Battle Points

On each bead, pray to support one of these good intentions:

- For the Holy Father and bishops, who define and defend the truth
- For catechists, theologians, and religion teachers
- For preachers
- For evangelists and apologists
- For parish directors of faith formation
- For Catholic writers, journalists, and media workers
- For ecumenical and interfaith workers
- For those being persecuted for their faith
- For the return of those who have left the Catholic faith
- For the conversion of atheists and false teachers

After the Fátima Prayer

Heavenly Father, your Son, Jesus Christ, is the Way, the Truth, the Life, and the Light. Strengthen your Church to do his work of teaching the truth of God in the world. Deliver us from false teachers and prophets. Protect our children from the lure of counterfeit religions and false teachings that would draw them away from Christ and endanger their souls. Fill the teachers of your truth with the Holy Spirit and guide them further into the truth of Christ the Teacher. Amen.

Wedding at Cana

Sins Against Marriage

(John 2:1-11)

A Jewish wedding in Jesus' day could be a weeklong celebration. The whole village of extended family and friends would gather to rejoice at the beginning of love and the hope of new life. Jesus' presence at the wedding in Cana is quiet. His light is glimmering as he shares in the wedding celebrations. He doesn't take center stage, and he even seems to indicate to his mother that he should remain in the background. Nevertheless, when the wine runs out, he quietly and confidently produces a supernatural supply of wine for the marriage feast. The beam of his radiant love and light fills the event with a supernatural grace. By his presence, he takes ordinary marriage into a new dimension as the water is transformed into wine.

The Dark Distortion

From the very beginning, God made marriage for men and women to learn the difficult lessons of love. Marriage is designed for one man and one woman for life. That's because it takes a lifetime to really learn how to give ourselves completely in love. Through his presence in the sacrament of Matrimony, Jesus Christ makes marriage a channel of grace. Marriage is therefore one of the ladders to heaven, because through marriage we learn how to love — and as St. John teaches, those who live in love live in God, and God lives in them" (1 Jn 4:16). Consequently, from his encounter with the first married couple — Adam and Eve — Satan has hated love and despised marriage. Because, through marriage, we learn how to give of ourselves and be faithful in love, Satan will do everything in his power to destroy marriage. In a wide range of ways, he distorts and destroys the precious and fragile gift of marriage.

Sexual promiscuity, fornication, and cohabitation distort marriage by dispensing with the faithfulness required in marriage. Adultery destroys the trust that makes a marriage strong. Divorce breaks a bond that is not to be broken. Emotional, psychological, and physical abuse bring violence into what should be a relationship of lifelong love. Pornography and prostitution pollute marriage, while same-sex "marriage," polyamory, and bigamy distort and destroy true marriage. Incest, rape, sexual abuse, and perversion pollute, distort, and destroy the purity and sanctity of marriage.

In all these ways, Satan tramples on the purity of the marriage bond, shatters the fragile bond of marriage, and shreds the precious gift of love between husband and wife.

Witnesses from the Battle

Janet discovered her husband's habit when she happened to read a secret journal he had in his desk drawer. Although they had three young children, and David worked as a pastor and youth-group leader, he had a dark, secret life. He was addicted to violent and risky sex with prostitutes.

Meanwhile, another man came to talk to me. James was a successful oral surgeon. Married with five children, he was shocked as he told me that his wife of twenty years announced that he had to leave the family home. She decided that she had to "find herself" and had found a twenty-five-year-old boy-friend. The divorce was long, bitter, and ugly.

Marriage in our society, and in our churches and families, is in crisis. Older couples are giving up on marriage. Younger men and women aren't even bothering. Like every revolution, the sexual revolution has been violent. Victims of this violent revolution are everywhere: abandoned wives and husbands, children without parents, and children who are learning to live with a second or third "father" or "mother."

The Church is there not to condemn, but to rescue the walking wounded from the battle — and our prayers are not only for married couples but also for all those who have been wounded in this great war for true love.

Meditate for Victory

Jesus' light in the heart of the marriage crisis is the quiet and confident light he showed at the Wedding at Cana. His love and mercy are a light that is strong and sure, like a lighthouse shining its beacon across the stormy sea of modern marriage.

Can you see him at the wedding feast, next to his Blessed Mother and surrounded by his disciples? That is a picture of the Church, which, St. Paul says, is like an immaculate and pure bride (Eph 5:27). The presence of Christ fills marriage with strength and purpose. The presence of his pure and spotless mother is a constant source of strength and inspiration to the married. She is full of grace, full of love, full of purity, and full of power to assist us in the great adventure of marriage.

The mercy of Christ is always available to heal and forgive our failures in marriage. Can you see the woman taken in adultery? (Jn 8:3-11). As you meditate on the mystery of marriage, meditate also on how Jesus responds to those who have failed in the great challenge of marriage. His love makes up for all that is lacking in their love. He does not condemn, but he also says with great tenderness and understanding, "Go, and do not sin again" (Jn 8:11).

Battle Points

On each bead, pray to support one of these good intentions:

- For couples preparing for marriage
- For those who teach marriage-preparation classes
- For marriage counselors
- For those who are struggling in their marriage
- For newlyweds
- For those who long to be married
- For those who seek forgiveness for sins committed against marriage
- For those who work on marriage tribunals
- For those who counsel the widowed and the divorced
- For those who struggle with sexual problems

After the Fátima Prayer

Father in heaven, your Son, Jesus Christ, sanctified marriage by his attendance at a wedding in Cana. Strengthen our commitment to marriage as the sacrament in which we learn how to love. Deliver us and our families from all the temptations that destroy and distort your precious gift of marriage. Through this sacrament, lead us to heaven, and draw us into your everlasting love. Amen.

Preaching the Kingdom
Illness and Disease
(Mark 1:14-15)

Can you picture Jesus in the prime of his life and ministry? He is working at his optimum, fulfilling God's call to preach the truth, heal the sick, and bring forgiveness and freedom to those in bondage. The crowds are gathering, and his fame is growing. The people are demanding. This person wants to be healed, that person has questions, and another person simply wants his attention. At this point, we see Jesus as a fully grown man, radiating confidence, self-knowledge, and a deep inner wisdom. He knows how to be with people, and he knows how to be alone. He weeps with those who weep and laughs with those who laugh. In his radiance, he shows us the glory of God: a human being fully alive. Jesus at work is Adam restored — the Son of God and a whole and perfect human being.

The Dark Distortion

The second-century theologian St. Irenaeus said, "The glory of God is a human being fully alive." Jesus shows us that glory of God in his perfection, and in doing so he reveals what each one of us should be. We should be healthy, happy, healed, and whole. We should be using our gifts to the fullest extent in service of God and others. We should be secure in ourselves

— humble and yet confident, standing tall on our own because our feet are planted on the rock that is Jesus Christ. Our body, mind, and spirit should be integrated, whole, and at peace.

Because of the curse of sin, however, our lives are broken and battered. We suffer from illness and disease, not only of the body but also of the mind and spirit. Spiritually, we are alienated from God, the source of life and love. Our souls are starved for union with God, and the symptoms are deep despair, loneliness, spiritual confusion, and fear. We wander in the darkness of our lives, like children lost in a chaotic and cacophonous city. We need to find peace. We need to find our way home.

Our minds are also sick. Confused by the noise and seduction of an entertainment culture — and bewildered by false philosophies, the lies of Satan, and distraction by the cares of the world — our minds are weighed down with confusion, fear, guilt, and depression. When these problems become acute, they surface in all forms of mental illness.

Our bodies reflect the sickness of our minds and spirits. We suffer from all sorts of physical ailments — many of them caused by an intemperate lifestyle, increased tension, worry, and stress. Wracked by disease and hit by environmental and societal forces beyond our control, our bodies, minds, and spirits are burdened by an overwhelming evil.

Witnesses from the Battle

Frank called the parish office: "I need to see a Catholic priest. It's urgent."

So I made my way to a rundown apartment complex and found Frank alone in a darkened room that smelled heavily of cigarette smoke. Frank said, "Are you a Catholic priest?"

"I am," I answered.

"Good, because the sisters said when you're dying call a priest. I'm dying so I called you."

"Well, here I am. Tell me, Frank, where do you go to church?"

"Church, Father? I haven't been to church for thirty years."

So I heard Frank's confession and talked to him about his future and his past. His life had been one long story of bad choices, deliberate sin, alienation from all his family and friends, and a string of disasters and tragedies. His lung cancer was the final illness in a life of dissipation, disease, and disappointment.

The next week I anointed Frank and visited him on his deathbed.

He looked up at me and gasped, "Well, I'm here all alone, Father. I'm dying alone, and I deserve it. I treated everyone else in my life real bad, and they're not here for me. I'm alone."

"No. You're not alone, Frank. I'm here, and do you remember this?" I held up my rosary.

"I do."

"Do you remember the Hail Mary?"

"Yep. The sisters taught me."

I gave him my rosary, "Then hold on to this. You're not alone. Jesus and Mary are with you. You've made your peace. You've made your confession. You're good to go."

So Frank died the next week. His body was ravaged by disease and death, but his soul was triumphant as he held on to the chain that linked him to Jesus the healer and his mother, Mary.

Meditate for Victory

It is wonderful to read the stories of Jesus healing the sick. The combination of physical healing and the forgiveness of sin reminds us that Jesus comes not simply to take away physical pains and illnesses but also to heal the sin-sick soul. As you visualize Jesus healing, see his power, not only to restore the body but also to reconcile the soul to God.

The mystery of the Lord's healing power and the reality of disease and death will hit all of us in one way or another, sooner or later. What words can we say to those who are in the midst of the battle with some horrible illness, chronic pain, or imminent death? Platitudes about Jesus' healing love don't help much.

Instead it helps to visualize Jesus healing the sick and raising his friend Lazarus. But as we do this, we should also meditate on the fact that there were many places where he could do no miracles because of people's lack of faith. Try to see his frustration and sadness at their lack of faith. Try to also see the radiance of his power and love as he still wants to reach out to bring healing, comfort, and strength to those who suffer.

Battle Points

On each bead, pray to support one of these good intentions:

- For the sick and suffering
- For doctors and nurses
- For auxiliary health-care workers
- For those doing medical research
- For psychiatrists and psychologists
- For those with the gift of spiritual healing
- For priests who exercise Christ's healing gifts in confession and anointing
- For those who care for the mentally ill

- For those who work with the disabled
- For those who care for the chronically ill

After the Fátima Prayer

Loving, heavenly Father, your Son came among us to
heal, forgive, and free us from bondage. Strengthen
and encourage all those who work in the healing
professions. Walk with those who suffer, and give
them hope. Drive far from us the spirit of disease,
sickness, and death. And by the power of your Holy
Spirit, restore your people to the fullness of health
and wholeness. Amen.

Transfiguration

Identity Confusion

(Luke 9:28-31)

Peter, James, and John see Jesus as their friend, the prophet who was once the carpenter from Nazareth. When Jesus takes them up Mount Tabor, they have no idea what they are going to see. Suddenly, their eyes are opened, and they see Jesus as he really is. The carpenter's son from Nazareth is transfigured, and he appears in radiant glory with Moses and Elijah from the Old Testament. For a moment, they not only see Jesus as he really is, but they also see everything else in the light of his presence. They see the essence of Jesus' whole being, and by that vision they feel more fully the sinful condition at the core of their being, and they respond the only way they can: with worship.

The Dark Distortion

St. John writes, "Beloved, we are God's children now; it does not yet appear what we shall be, but we know that when he appears we shall be like him, for we shall see him as he is" (1 Jn 3:2). In his first letter to the Christians at Corinth, St. Paul says: "For now we see in a mirror dimly, but then face to face. Now I know in part; then I shall understand fully, even as I have been fully understood" (1 Cor 13:12). In the Transfiguration, the disciples had a glimpse of glory. They saw the true identity of Jesus, and in seeing him they saw who they really were. This is our ultimate destiny: to become real at last, to become whole and complete in Christ.

This life is a time to grow up into the person God created us to be. To be purged of our faults and to become mature and complete in Christ is the hard work of a lifetime. To be complete in Christ is to be a saint, and Satan hates the prospect of there being even one more saint in the world.

He tempts us to avoid that great quest and escape into being someone else. Because of our insecurities, we try to emulate other people. We copy friends and acquaintances. We try to be like a celebrity or someone we envy. We lie about our accomplishments. We put on airs and graces. We brag and strut. We adopt different clothes and appearances. Out of vanity, we have cosmetic surgery and body enhancements, and we buy expensive clothes, trying to appear better on the outside than we really are.

In our sick society, there are others who are even more deeply confused about their identity. Through mobility, broken families, and broken society, many have no roots, no family, and are therefore confused about who they are and what their purpose in life should be. Not knowing who they are or what life is for, they drift into crime, seek comfort in substance abuse, or seek love through promiscuity or prostitution. Others, for complicated reasons, are confused about their gender. They don't know if they are men or women. They don't know how to adjust or where to fit in. They are often lonely and confused, trying on many different identities like a different set of clothes each day.

Witnesses from the Battle

"Sam" was the right name for her because Samantha wasn't sure if she was a man or a woman. Sam's father left home before she ever had a chance to know him, and her mother — broken and disappointed by the men in her life — decided that she was really a lesbian. She started living with a woman who had been raped by her father and uncles from a young age.

Sam was brought up by two women who had a deep hatred for men. When she started dating, they mocked her for liking boys. Wounded by that experience, she began to experiment with lesbian partners. I got to know Sam when she was in college, and by then she had had numerous friends, sexual partners, and live-in lovers of both sexes. It was no wonder she was confused. Was she straight or gay? Was she really supposed to be a woman, or was she a man trapped in a woman's body? She wasn't sure.

In a strange way, her lack of identity was not that different from Jayson's. Coming from a broken home, Jayson's African American mother put him up for adoption. A white family took him in, but in high school his black friends said he was "too white," while his white friends didn't understand why he was hanging around with black gang members. Jayson didn't have any roots and had no way to discover and celebrate his true identity.

Jayson and Sam needed to realize that the search for reality and one's true identity is a lifetime's task. Growing into who we really are is the task of each one of us, and it is only when we find Christ — who is reality itself — that we will eventually also come to find and accept ourselves.

Can the simple prayer of the Rosary help us grow into our full and true identity? I'm convinced that it can, because as we pray the Rosary we identify deeply with Jesus the God-man and Mary — the truest and most complete of God's created beings.

Meditate for Victory

In your imagination, be with the disciples on the Mount of Transfiguration. For a moment, picture Jesus as the carpenter from Nazareth or as the gentle person healing the sick and teaching the crowds. See him tired and hungry after a long day. See him alone with God in the wilderness. Now on the mountain, see him transfigured. He is radiant with light and glowing with power, goodness, simplicity, and love.

This is what the Transfiguration means: to see Jesus for who he really is — and in his light, to see light. Imagine the radiance of the transfigured Lord filling your whole life and allowing you to see more clearly those things that are darkened to you. Imagine his light helping you to see with clarity your own vanity, self-deception, false image, and pride. Allow his light to reveal also who you really are. Ask to see your true gifts, your true abilities, and your huge potential.

For you to go on this journey is the first step toward understanding how confused, lonely, and alienated so many people are in our society today. Going on this journey is the path to humility. The poet T. S. Eliot said, "The only wisdom we can hope to acquire / Is the wisdom of humility: humility is endless."

Now imagine this clarity, wholeness, and humility of Christ radiating not only into your own life but also into the lives of those who are broken, lost, and confused about their heritage, their identity, and their destiny. See the whole and complete God-man, Jesus Christ, reaching out to them with healing and wholeness in his embrace.

Battle Points

On each bead, pray to support one of these good intentions:

- For parents and grandparents
- For orphans and those from broken homes
- For counselors and psychologists

- For people who are confused about gender identities
- For immigrants and those without a country
- For those with mental and identity disorders
- For the homeless and the unemployed
- For those who block out the pain of their own identity
- For those who hide behind a vain and false image
- For those who have no spiritual identity or home

After the Fátima Prayer

Heavenly Father, at the Transfiguration your Son
revealed his true glory, the glory as of the only-
begotten of the Father. Help us to see ourselves as
you have made us. Remove the scales of vanity and
pride from our lives, and teach us humility. Heal all
those who suffer from confusion, fear, and loneliness
because they do not know who they are and what
their lives are for. Help us to welcome them and
introduce them to Christ the Lord, who to know is
life itself. Amen.

Institution of the Eucharist
Division and Hatred of the Sacred
(John 6:51; 10:10)

The humble upper room is the scene. Jesus is gathered with his closest friends for their final meal together. As they celebrate the Passover, the apostles are united with one another and with the Lord. Looking to the past, they are united with all the Jewish believers since Moses' time, and, looking to the future, they are united with the billions of souls who will celebrate this Eucharist until the end of time. Can you sense the fellowship they share around the table? God is in their midst. Heaven is on earth for a time. The sacred is alive in their ordinary lives. In ways far more profound than they could then understand, they were becoming one with the body of Christ, and they were joining themselves with Christ's one, full, final sacrifice and with his whole Church around the world and down the ages.

The Dark Distortion

The Eucharist is the sacrament of unity. St. Paul writes, "We who are many are one body, for we all partake of the one bread" (1 Cor 10:17). The Eucharist is not only the sacrament of unity for the Church, but it is also a focus of unity for all believers. The unity of the Church is the seedbed for the unity of the whole world, but that unity is broken by hatred, strife, selfishness, division, and hatred of the sacred.

Satan bitterly hates the Eucharist. Satanists admit that in their dark rituals they intentionally blaspheme and desecrate a consecrated host from a Catholic Mass. Hatred of the sacred and revulsion at the Eucharist may be signs of true demonic possession, but hatred of the sacred Eucharist is not limited to those who are obviously possessed.

Many more hate the Catholic Church and Jesus Christ. Radical Protestants and hateful members of other religions despise the Catholic Church and all we hold sacred. Atheists mock the faith, and secularists do all they can to undermine, distort, and destroy what Catholics hold sacred. Those separated from God's love descend into the murky underworld of irrational rage, hatred, and violence of hell.

The irrational rage that burns in the heart of humanity is the twisted condition of a race alienated from God and rebellious against the very power that would reconcile that race to his love. That irrational rage erupts in all forms of division, war, strife, violence, and destruction. Having turned away from the source of life, light, and love, they go on a fearful rampage in actions that are the very opposite of the peace, forgiveness, brotherhood, and joy that is made real in the Eucharist.

In its ultimate form, this separation from God ends in demonic obsession, oppression, and possession. Individual souls become locked in fierce rebellion, hating God and everything sacred. They are allied not with God but with Satan, and he has control of their whole being.

Witnesses from the Battle

Father Emmanuel is an exorcist, and he tells the story of the man he met in the hospital for the criminally insane.

Bruce was a murderer. He had killed three men in a terrible, irrational fit of fury. Father Emmanuel said whenever he went into the hospital to celebrate Mass, Bruce would be waiting for him, hissing and spitting like a cornered wildcat — ready to attack.

Bruce's irrational fear and rage in the presence of a priest made Father Emmanuel wonder if the man's personality had been taken over by demonic powers. When he learned more about Bruce, Father Emmanuel realized that the man's whole life had been given over to dark forces. It was as if he was a slave to Satan. Through Christ's power and Father Emmanuel's ministry, Bruce was finally delivered from the evil that controlled him.

Bruce's case is an extreme example of how evil can take over and a hatred of the sacred can develop. There are many more people who have given themselves to the darkness, who gradually slip away from God and his grace, until at last they find themselves mocking and scorning the Lord who would save them.

Bruce's hatred of Christ and his Church can also be seen on the corporate level. Throughout history, we can see how whole nations are overwhelmed by the powers of darkness, erupting into a wave of violence against Christ, his Church, and his sacraments. From the early persecutions of the Church to the violence of the English Reformation, the French Revolution, anti-Catholic violence in Mexico, the Spanish Civil War, and the oppression of the Church by communists, we have seen the murder of priests and religious, the destruction of churches, the prohibition of Mass, and the attempt to eradicate Christianity completely.

Can the Holy Rosary be an effective weapon against such hate? Yes. Our Lady of Victories is a celebration of the power of Christ's light over the darkness, but such victories are not won without much prayer and the sacrifice of self-giving.

Meditate for Victory

In this Luminous mystery, see the quiet light of the lamps that night at the Last Supper. They connect with the ever-burning sanctuary lamps in our Catholic churches, indicating that Christ the Lord is present. It is this Eucharistic presence of Christ that is alive in the world, and which keeps the world from disintegrating into a cesspit of violence, bloodshed, war, demonic division, and strife.

See the unity that Jesus has with his apostles. This connects with the unity we share as members of the one, holy, catholic, and apostolic Church. This mystical unity is affirmed and confirmed every day as countless priests and people around the world celebrate Mass.

As you meditate on the mystery of the Mass and the Lord's presence in the Eucharist, bring forward in prayer the strife, division, rage, and hatred of the sacred that may exist in your family, in your community, in your country, and in the world. See the healing light of Christ radiating from his Eucharistic presence, and thank God, remembering that the word *Eucharist* means "thanksgiving."

As you see the light of Christ at the Eucharist, see that light radiating out to touch those who are locked in the darkness of demonic oppression. Pray for that light to reach them by the mercy of God.

Battle Points

On each bead, pray to support one of these good intentions:

- For the pope, bishops, and priests
- For deacons and religious

- For an increase in vocations to the priesthood
- For exorcists and ministers of healing
- For those possessed by demons
- For those trapped in violence, division, and hatred
- For those who hate Christ and his Church
- For those who work for religious freedom
- For peace to reign in the heart of humanity
- For an increase in Eucharistic Adoration

After the Fátima Prayer

Father in heaven, you sent your Son to bring peace
to the world by reconciling a rebellious race to
your everlasting love. In the Eucharist, he left a
memorial of his sacrifice of peace and established his
Eucharistic presence on earth until the end of time.
Deliver us from all hatred of the sacred, and from
the division, strife, and violence that result from our
hatred of you and your love. Make us ministers of
reconciliation, and grant us your peace. Amen.

III.

The Sorrowful Mysteries

Agony in the Garden

Doubt, Fear, and Persecution

(Luke 22:39-42)

In the Garden of Gethsemane, everything seems lost. Jesus faces the dark night of the soul. His disciples have fallen asleep. Satan is attacking, and Jesus is wracked with doubt and fear. He knows the only way forward is torture and death but pleads for there to be some other way. More than the fear of physical pain and the agony of death, Jesus faces the pain of misunderstanding, loneliness, and betrayal — and, beyond this, the devil's wish to make him feel worthless. Jesus is tempted to believe that the battle has all been in vain, and that his enemies will triumph; that all the good he has tried to do has been wasted; that all the truth he has tried to live is now spat upon; that all the love he has tried to give is now rejected. He does know, for certain, that he faces torture and death from many of the very ones he has tried to help.

The Dark Distortion

God created us to live in loving, trusting harmony with him. Because we are his children, he wants us to be confident and full of hope. To dwell in his love is to abide without fear.

Satan hates the idea that we should dwell in such a state of harmony and union with God. He breaks that harmony through fear. St. John teaches, "Perfect love casts out fear" (1 Jn 4:18). It follows that fear comes from the absence of perfect love. Because of our frail human condition, Satan first gets us to doubt God's perfect love, and that doubt leads to the lack of love, which results in fear. Fear then grows like a cancer into all sorts of negativities: anger, rage, blaming others, verbal violence, and finally physical violence, injuries, and even death.

Part of the curse of fear is the temptation to blame others for our problems. When we blame others, we are locked in the dark dynamic of scapegoating. If others are to blame for our problems, then to get rid of our problems we must get rid of the ones we think are causing the problems. First, we ostracize and mock them. Then, we isolate and expel. Finally, we imprison and kill the ones we think are to blame. The human race is plunged into this darkness, doubt, and fear, and it is this intense darkness and isolation that Jesus faces in his agony in the Garden of Gethsemane.

Witnesses from the Battle

James was brimming with anger. Everything in his life was wrong, and everybody else was to blame. He was mad at his boss and frustrated in his dead-end job. He was angry with his wife because she had given up on him. He was mad at the police, the government, and the media. He blamed his teachers, his parents, his friends, and family members. Increasingly, he was escaping from his anger, rage, and depression with alcohol.

Then he found a group of people he could blame for his problems. It was the Christians. A confident and happy group of men at work were churchgoers, and James started to blame them for his failures and disappointments. Christians have been the object of rage and blame from the time of the first martyr, St. Stephen (Acts 6 and 7). The powers of darkness have plunged the enemies of Christ into the cycle of doubt, fear, and blame, and Satan convinces them that the followers of Jesus Christ are to blame for their problems.

There were more Christian martyrs in the twentieth century than in all the other centuries combined, and the persecution of Christians does not look as if it is about to ease up. Christians are persecuted by Muslims, Hindus, and Buddhists. Christians are blamed by corrupt politicians, gangsters, criminals, and dictatorial regimes.

Christians are persecuted around the world, but in the Middle East they have been under special attack for a long time. They are denied employment, subjected to bureaucratic harassment, and driven from their homes and schools. Their churches, buildings, seminaries, monasteries, and convents are bulldozed. In the worst attacks, the women are sold as slaves, the men are butchered, and the children and their mothers are imprisoned.

Meditate for Victory

The Sorrowful Mysteries take us, with Christ, into the very heart of darkness. In each of these mysteries, as we identify with Christ's sufferings, we will also identify with the sufferings of his precious body, the Church.

Can you hear Jesus' groans of agony? The Gospel says that in his doubt, fear, and loneliness, he sweated blood. This is not just a symbol. Sweating blood occurs when a person is under extreme stress and the agony of fear. The condition has been noted among people waiting on death row, just before their execution. Jesus' agony is that of all those who are locked in Satan's prison of doubt, fear, and blame.

As you see Jesus being tormented by the darkness, see how his suffering gathers up the suffering of those who are persecuted for the faith. They are the victims of the doubt, fear, and blame that come from alienation from God. For your own healing, offer up to God any doubt, fear, and blame that darkens your own memory, your own heart, and your own relationships with others. Join your sufferings with the fear that Christ felt, and let him gather up your anxiety into his.

Battle Points

On each bead, pray to support one of these good intentions:

- For healing for those who are locked in depression, rage, and fear
- For those troubled with doubt
- For all who are rejected by family and friends
- For all who imagine that they are unloved
- For psychiatrists, psychologists, and counselors
- For reconciliation for all who are alienated from God's love and forgiveness
- For forgiveness for those who blame others because of their race, religion, or ethnicity
- For priests who minister to those locked in doubt, fear, and rage
- For those threatened by persecution
- For legislators and soldiers who battle against persecutors

After the Fátima Prayer

Father in heaven, it is your will that we live in peace and trusting harmony with you and with our neighbor. Deliver us from Satan's darkness of fear, suspicion, rage, and hatred. Protect all Christians from those who would project onto them their rage and blame them for their problems. Save them from the pains and perils of persecution. This we pray by virtue of our Lord's sorrowful passion. Amen.

Scourging at the Pillar

Imprisonment and Torture

(Matthew 27:26)

The scourges that the Romans used were strips of leather with shards of metal or broken pottery tied onto them. They ripped into the flesh and tore strips off the victim's back. Jesus is sent out to be flogged, not as a punishment but as an act of deliberate torture to appease the crowd. He takes not only the physical pain but also the mental and emotional anguish of being punished for something he never did. It is easy to say that we are healed through his suffering, and redeemed by his passion. It is much harder to enter the mystery and experience what this means. As you meditate on his Sorrowful Mysteries, allow the Holy Spirit to take you into an understanding of Christ's experience of the darkness that is beyond words.

The Dark Distortion

"Where the spirit of the Lord is, there is freedom" (2 Cor 3:17), and the Lord declared:

The Spirit of the Lord is upon me,
because he has anointed me to preach good news
to the poor.

He has sent me to proclaim release to the captives
and recovery of sight to the blind,
to set at liberty those who are the oppressed. (Lk 4:18)

Freedom and confidence are signs of a Spirit-filled follower of Jesus Christ.

But Satan hates freedom. He hates freedom because it is through the free exercise of the human will that we can obey God and come to truly know and love him. Because it is through freedom that a person can learn to love, Satan wants to destroy freedom in all its forms.

He destroys spiritual freedom by tempting, trapping, imprisoning, and tormenting people through slavery to sin. He enslaves people through addictions, and he erodes the freedom of our will through continued indulgence in sin. He destroys mental freedom by lies, false teaching, heresy, and blasphemy. In every way, Satan wants to enslave us so that we will serve him instead of God.

Knowing that he will be imprisoned and tormented forever in hell, Satan wants to drag as many people as possible down to those torture chambers of Gehenna. Not content with spiritual imprisonment and torture, Satan will also do whatever possible to enchain people in the slavery of poverty, the slavery of fear, and the slavery of bitterness, anger, and regret.

Through unjust punishment and persecution, he will try to lock up the innocent; and by temptations to commit crimes, Satan will be delighted to lock up as many people as possible and throw away the keys. Because he hates freedom, Satan delights in cruelty, imprisonment, and torture of every kind.

Witnesses from the Battle

Edmund Campion was a brilliant young student at Oxford during the reign of the Protestant Queen Elizabeth I. While at Oxford, he converted from the Anglican religion and left England to train as a Jesuit missionary priest. After his training, he returned to England and served the Catholics at a time when every Catholic priest in England was being hunted down as a spy and traitor. The punishment for saying Mass in England at the time was death.

Campion was finally captured and taken to the Tower of London, where he was imprisoned in a tiny cell and tortured on the rack — a cruel instrument by which a person was slowly stretched until the body literally started to tear apart. He never gave in, and he defended his Catholic faith with intellectual brilliance, wit, and compassion.

Edmund Campion's unjust imprisonment, torture, and martyrdom were his own identification with the sufferings of Christ. As a prisoner and victim of torture, he is also a witness to all who are imprisoned in any way — both those who are guilty and those who are innocent.

Meditate for Victory

Jesus' being held as a prisoner and being flogged at the pillar is the sign of his complete identification with all those who have lost their freedom and are tortured by their own evil choices and by those who hate them. In this mystery, Jesus goes down into the depths of prison, torture, and anguish to rescue the lost sons and daughters of Eve.

As you pray this mystery, do not avoid the gruesome vision of Jesus enduring the most cruel and heartless torture at the hands of the Roman soldiers. Identifying with Jesus' passion helps us to remember in prayer all those who are victims of torture and unjust punishment — especially our Christian brothers and sisters who are imprisoned for their faith.

As you meditate on Jesus' loss of freedom and cruel torture, also bring to mind all prisoners, no matter what they have done. Remember also those who are locked in the prison house of addiction and slavery to their own sinful choices. Christ came to rescue them as well, and his suffering love can reach down even to the darkest prison and the human heart locked in the darkest bondage.

Battle Points

On each bead, pray to support one of these good intentions:

- For prisoners
- For prison chaplains
- For prison officers
- For judges and lawyers
- For those who are imprisoned unjustly
- For those who face deprivation or torture
- For those who rehabilitate prisoners
- For those who are in bondage to addictions
- For those who help addicts break free
- For those who are in bondage to Satan

After the Fátima Prayer

Heavenly Father, you sent your Son, Jesus Christ, to set prisoners free. Strengthen and encourage all who minister in our prisons. Help judges and lawyers to administer justice tempered with mercy. Deliver our leaders from the temptation to use cruelty, violence, or torture in their treatment of prisoners. Deliver those in bondage to addictions. Most of all, deliver us from all that keeps us in chains spiritually. Help us to overcome our slavery to sin, and by your Holy Spirit, set us free. Amen.

Crowning with Thorns

Mockery, Humiliation, and Abuse of the Poor

(Matthew 27:28-31)

With his body broken and bleeding, the cruel soldiers pull Jesus up from the terrible scourging and proceed to mock him as the King of the Jews. The purple cloak they hang about him is the color the emperor wears. They weave a crown of thorns, press it onto his head, and push a broken stick into his hand as a mock scepter. Shoving him to and fro, the soldiers mock and humiliate the one who is their Lord and God. The crown of thorns and humiliating signs of royalty hurt even more because Jesus knows he is the Lord of glory, but he says nothing.

The Dark Distortion

Every human person is created in the image of God. We therefore have innate dignity as eternal souls. We are blessed and granted dignity simply by being his sons and daughters. That he sent his own Son to take human flesh from a young virgin consolidated his image in us. We were made in his image, and his Son was made in our image. This innate dignity is the natural human right of every man, woman, boy, and girl.

But Satan hates our human dignity with a passionate hatred. He despised Adam and Eve at the beginning, and he hates each one of us for being created in God's image. He hates the Blessed Virgin Mary, he spits on the dignity that each one of us shares in being human, but he especially hates those who have been baptized and who are being remade in the image and likeness of Christ the King.

Therefore, Satan will do everything he can to distort and twist that innate human dignity. He loves to push us down and shove our noses in our weaknesses. He mocks and humiliates us through our bondage to sin. He lowers us when we suffer from sickness, mental illness, addiction, and homelessness. When we are down and out, he revels in our humiliation. When we are poor refugees or impoverished immigrants, he delights in our suffering, our humiliation, and our poverty.

Satan uses his agents in the world to humiliate others further. When the rich and the powerful mock and ignore the weak and the poor, Satan is pleased. When immigrants and refugees are humiliated further by being rejected and forced into poverty, Satan is happy. When the homeless, the hungry, the mentally ill, the sick, and the suffering are humiliated by their plight, Satan delights further when those who are not suffering ignore them and refuse to come to their aid.

Wherever a human being is deprived of simple respect and dignity, wherever a human being is humiliated, mocked, and scorned — Satan is happy.

Witnesses from the Battle

One of the most moving experiences I ever had was to visit one of Mother Teresa's homes in El Salvador. The little nun, Sister Cecilia, was so happy that a team of high school kids and I were paying a visit. She explained how the residents of her home were mentally disabled adults whom nobody else wanted.

All had been rejected by their families and had been living on the street. Some were born with mental defects. Others suffered from mental problems because of drugs. Others were mentally ill or emotionally disturbed. They lived together in a simple Christian community, sharing their humble meals and working as a family. Each morning they worshipped together at Mass, and every evening they prayed the Rosary.

The day we visited, Sister had arranged for her little family of "misfits" to have a dance. One of our students was a handsome young man named Michael. I'll never forget when he went up to a woman whose mind was ravaged by drugs and asked her to dance. She broke into a huge toothless smile, and Michael danced with her. Sister Cecilia whispered to me, "Her name is Ana Maria. She has spent her life as a prostitute, and her brain is damaged from drugs."

The people in Mother Teresa's home in El Salvador had had their natural human dignity torn away from them through the horrors of life on the street and by the cruelty of their family and friends. Sister Cecilia and Michael saw their dignity, and in a simple embrace showed that they were still children of God.

Meditate for Victory

In this Sorrowful mystery, think how terrible it would be to have your dignity torn away from you. What is it that gives you your self-worth and makes you proud to be a son or daughter of the heavenly Father? What if that were taken from you?

Imagine Jesus, the King of kings and Lord of lords, being beaten and humiliated by the soldiers who had no idea what they were doing. He who was the very source of dignity, goodness, and life was kicked around, mocked, and scorned. As Jesus' dignity was stripped away, he identified completely with all those whose innate human dignity has been demolished.

See Jesus' suffering and meditate on what he endured. His dignity was shattered so that ours might be restored. The very image of God in man and man in God was broken, despised, and humiliated so that we might recover the dignity of the sons and daughters of God.

Battle Points

On each bead, pray to support one of these good intentions:

- For the poor and those who help them
- For the homeless and those who help them
- For the unemployed and those who help them
- For refugees, immigrants, and those who help them
- For those rejected by their family and friends
- For those who suffer from mental illness or mental defects and for those who help them
- For the disabled, the wounded, the chronically ill, and those who help them
- For those who work for peace and justice on behalf of the oppressed
- For those who are wrongly accused
- For those who work to defend human rights

After the Fátima Prayer

Our loving, heavenly Father, each one of us is created in your image, with infinite worth and noble dignity. Comfort and support all those who are humiliated by their situation in life. Defend them from the strong and the arrogant who would push them down further with mockery and cruelty. Strengthen and encourage all those who work for human rights and for justice for the poor, and help us to treat each person as our brother and sister in Christ. Amen.

Carrying the Cross
War, Gangs, and Mob Violence
(Luke 23:26-32)

The soldiers pull off Jesus' purple robe and lash the heavy, rough-hewn crossbeam to his shoulders for the next stage of torture. As the mob howls with rage, mockery, and hatred, the condemned men carry their own crosses through the crowded streets. As the crowd bays for blood, they shift all their fear, guilt, and anger onto the criminals. As Jesus is pushed and shoved by the crowd, he falls under the weight, and the cross crushes him to the ground. Fearing that he may pass out or die before he can be crucified, the soldiers force Simon of Cyrene to take up Jesus' cross. The Gospel says that Simon follows Jesus as he makes his way through the furious mob, up to the hill of execution.

The Dark Distortion

As beings created in God's image, we are imbued not only with innate dignity but also with free will and responsibility. As God is all powerful, so he gives us some of his power. We can make choices. When we are operating at our full potential as his creatures, we take responsibility for ourselves. Our decisions matter. We can choose good or evil. Part of that choice is admitting when we have chosen badly and deciding to do better the next time.

Satan hates it when we admit we were wrong. He howls with rage when we repent and say we are sorry for messing up. He snarls with fury when we ask for forgiveness and intend to do better. He hates repentance because he is proud and will never repent. When things go wrong, he wants us, instead of admitting it and asking for forgiveness, to blame others.

Blaming others is the heart of human darkness. Blaming others is the starkest symptom of pride. When we blame others, our freedom to take responsibility for ourselves is twisted completely. Blaming others leads us down a path of destruction and distortion of the truth.

When we blame others, we must follow the twisted logic and solve the problem by "getting rid" of that person or those people. On an individual level, we might rid ourselves of those we blame by ignoring them or isolating them. But when the blaming rises to the group level — whether mobs, tribes, or gangs — the behaviors can become extreme, even to the point of making plans to expel or kill the "offenders."

This is the dynamic we see as Jesus carries his cross through the howling mob, who are longing to see him killed.

Witnesses from the Battle

Padre Pepe is a Salesian priest who works in the slums of San Salvador city. He reclaimed a garbage dump to create a park, a technical school, a chapel, and a home for abandoned children.

Padre Pepe tells stories from the streets, where he comes face-to-face with the gang members that terrorize San Salvador's slums. The gangs of young men practice every kind of crime. Ordinary people have to pay protection money, or else they are attacked. Twelve-year-old boys are pressured to join the gangs, and their initiation ceremony is to kill someone.

The girls are forced into prostitution, while their parents watch helplessly.

The gang, the tribe, the mob — all of these are the devil's counterfeit for the family, the Church, the community of faith. An individual's dignity and free will is obliterated by the mob mentality, the forced conformity, and the threat of violence. The mob survives by finding an enemy to attack. Like voracious animals, they turn on the weakest and most vulnerable — and when mob violence occurs on a national and international scale, war is the result.

Gangs in the slums of big cities are not the only kind of poisonous group. A political party, a club, a social caste, or even a religious sect can become a dangerous tribe and a force for group evil.

It is only through courageous individuals like Padre Pepe that the crowd terror can be broken and reconciliation achieved. It is only through prayer and sacrifice that the family can replace the tribe, the community replace the mob, and the Body of Christ — the Church — replace the gang.

Meditate for Victory

As you meditate on this Sorrowful mystery, see Jesus taking on himself the mockery, cruelty, and senseless attack of the mob. As he drags his cross through the streets, hear their howls. See their mocking faces, and sense the stink of their sweat and the smell of their rage.

Jesus takes it all. Then see in this path of sorrow how Simon of Cyrene shares the cross of Christ. This is the role of each one who prays the Rosary for spiritual warfare. We walk with Christ and understand the depth of the darkness that he faced. We take up our cross and follow him, and so we help to bear the weight, carry the pain, and win the reconciliation and peace.

This is why we call Jesus the Prince of Peace — not because he is a lofty diplomat who negotiates a peace, but because he is a bloodied warrior who battles the Prince of darkness and wins the prize. The peace of Christ is not some weak and passive submission to evil. It is the peace that comes after a hard-won victory.

As you meditate on Jesus making his way to the mountain of sacrifice, see every step of his long, hard trek as one more sword stroke against our indomitable foe.

Battle Points

On each bead, pray to support one of these good intentions:

- For the strengthening of families, communities, and the Church
- For victims of gang violence
- For victims of war
- For those who work to save young people from gangs
- For police and law-enforcement officers
- For soldiers who fight in just wars
- For those wounded by war
- For diplomats and peacemakers
- For soldiers who are peacekeepers
- For the repose of the souls of those lost in battle

After the Fátima Prayer

Father in heaven, your Son, Jesus Christ, is the Prince
of Peace. Deliver us from the anti-family of mob
violence and the bloodshed of war. Strengthen and
encourage all who work for peace and true justice.
Help members of the military and police to protect
the peace, nurture security, and guard what fragile
peace there is. Deliver us from the curse of murdering
one another, and by your Holy Spirit, build us into
a community of peace, justice, and reconciliation, all
this for the sake of your Son, our Lord Jesus Christ.
Amen.

Crucifixion

Murder, Execution, and Genocide

(Matthew 27:33-50)

Jesus finally arrives at Golgotha — the place of the skull. Crucifixion is the worst form of torture and death because the victim remains suspended in agony, usually for days. As Jesus hangs on the cross, he is abandoned by all but his mother, the apostle John, and a few women disciples. Hanging naked, for the world to see, Jesus faces the final enemy in physical agony. His inner torment is even greater. He feels that his Father has also abandoned him, and he is tempted to despair and even to lose faith. Still, in the midst of his anguish, he is able to plead for forgiveness for his tormentors and to share his love and forgiveness with one who is crucified with him. Finally, it is finished, and his lifeless body hangs above a lonely world, a sign to all of the vulnerable power of God.

The Dark Distortion

Human life is a gift from God. Scientists can manipulate life, but they cannot create life. The indefinable breath we call life is God giving us the gift of himself. Because all human beings are created in God's image, that fire of life within us is, if you like, a little bit of immortality — and therefore a little bit of God.

Furthermore, God does not only wish for us to have life. Jesus says, "I have come that you might have life more abundantly" (cf. Jn 10:10). In other words, he wants us to have a good life, filled with love and overflowing with blessings. He wants us to have a life that is free, positive, and powerful in its goodness.

When I was a high school chaplain, I would say to my students, "You must understand that Satan hates you. He despises you. He wants you dead. He wants to devour you. He hates the very fact that you have life within you, and that, if you are a follower of Jesus Christ, you will live forever."

This is why the devil inspires all forms of killing. Murder, abortion, genocide, war, execution — all destroy human life. Through violence, he destroys life, and through sin he distorts the goodness of life. Hatred is the bitter desire to destroy another person's life — and refusing to forgive, bearing a grudge, and planning revenge are all quiet killers.

If Satan cannot get us to kill physically, he will tempt us to destroy the abundant life God promises. Many of the sins we fall into seem pleasurable at first, but have a sting in the tail because they distort the abundant and free life God promises, and eventually lead to death itself.

This is the death of the soul. Jesus said, "Do not fear those who kill the body but cannot kill the soul; rather fear him who can destroy both soul and body in hell" (Mt 10:28). The final dark distortion is Satan's victory, and it is this everlasting death that we should most fear.

Witnesses from the Battle

Jason was the first murderer I ever met.

When I was working in prison ministry in the United Kingdom, I got to know the guys who were in my rehab class, and finally in a private conversation Jason told me his story. As a teenager, he got in with the wrong crowd and soon moved on from taking drugs to dealing drugs.

It was when he was high one night that he argued with another drug dealer and, picking up a brick, bashed the other guy's head, killing him. By the time I met him, Jason had already served twenty years of a thirty-year sentence.

"I guess I got off easy because they thought it wasn't premeditated," he explained. He was silent for a moment and then continued:

> But I had been hating that guy for over a year, ever since he double-crossed me in a drug deal. I didn't exactly plan the murder, but I'd spent a long time hating him and wishing him dead. I guess that night I just acted out what had been in me for a long time.

Jason found God in prison. He found the Catholic faith. He found the Rosary, and he found peace and a whole new dimension to life. Because of his own faith and forgiveness, Jason spent much of his time working with the chaplain to help other prisoners find reconciliation and release.

Meditate for Victory

In the Middle Ages, the idea was popular of Jesus being a great warrior, with the cross as his battlefield. On the cross, he battled the ancient foe and trampled down the serpent. The enemy was the Dark Lord of Death itself.

There, as he is nailed to the tree and endures his final agony, see that he is enduring not only the physical pain but also the torment of being separated from the source of life and love. He is going into the realm of death, going into the great darkness, and it is this battle that is his greatest ordeal.

As you meditate on this Sorrowful mystery, draw to mind all those who are facing death by violence, all those who have committed acts of murder, and all those who are the victims of violence. As you see Christ's abundant life bruised, broken, and finally destroyed, see also how bitter hatred and refusal of forgiveness ultimately bring death and destruction.

Battle Points

On each bead, pray to support one of these good intentions:

- For victims of violence
- For the families of victims of violence
- For those who face death by execution, torture, or genocide
- For those who minister to prisoners on death row
- For those who protect others from violence
- For the spirit of forgiveness and reconciliation
- For those who are locked in bitter anger and seek revenge
- For peacemakers
- For those who minister to prisoners guilty of violent crime
- For the repose of the souls of those killed by violence

After the Fátima Prayer

Heavenly Father, you looked with great sorrow on
the death of your only-begotten Son, our Lord Jesus
Christ. He entered the darkness of death to win the
final victory, and he battled the Ancient Accuser to
bring reconciliation and forgiveness to all. Deliver
us from the spirit of hatred, bitterness, and revenge.
Drive far from us all violence and bloodshed, and
preserve your people in peace and in the abundant life
you promise. Amen.

IV.

The Glorious Mysteries

Resurrection

Pollution and Corruption

(Matthew 28:1-6)

Jesus can't stay dead. How can you kill Life itself? On the third day, his glory is manifested as he rises from the dead. His resurrection is the final victory over evil. As he bursts from the tomb on Easter morning, he tramples on suffering, pain, illness, and death once and for all. His victory is like a seed being planted in the history of the world. Once he rises from the dead, a new day dawns, not only for all of humanity but also for the whole of creation. His resurrection is the birthday of life, beauty, goodness, and truth. With the rising of the Son of God, the dignity, innocence, and majesty of God's whole creation also rises again.

The Dark Distortion

The early Church Fathers saw the resurrection of Jesus from the dead as "the eighth day." It was a new beginning, a new creation. The fallen old order was given a fresh start. The Resurrection brought new life to the whole world. The weary and worn human race could be children once again, and the whole created order was made new.

Satan howled with rage. He thought this created world belonged to him. He had already ruined it with violence, hatred, corruption, fear, and death. Now that the Son of God had risen from the dead, all his work was ruined. He hated the idea that humanity and all of creation was getting a fresh start.

That is why, from that time on, Satan has continued his timeless struggle to destroy and distort everything good that God has made. He does this with the deeply rooted malice and irrational violence of a nasty child pulling the wings off a fly or torturing a kitten. Satan hates the beauty, innocence, and goodness of a bright spring morning. He hates the natural order, and he hates the human race.

There are two ways he does this: he corrupts the innocent, and he pollutes and destroys nature. Wherever Satan sees innocence — in a child or in a person trying to be a saint — he attacks. Through lies, violence, sexual, mental, and physical abuse, Satan and the people who are under his control will corrupt the innocent, smear their natural trust, demolish their hope, and smash their joy. Whenever you see a child sexualized, abused, and hurt, you see the joy and innocence of Easter being destroyed.

The resurrection of Christ also brought new life to the whole created order. God has commanded the human race to be good stewards of his creation. We are therefore supposed to be like gardeners in a garden — full of love, respect, and joy in the innocent beauty of nature. Satan and those under his command rape and ravage the land. We humans destroy, pollute, and pillage for financial gain. We turn animals into meat and milk machines. We tinker with genetics, and we manipulate and distort the natural order for our own pleasure, wealth, and recreation. As the poet Gerard Manley Hopkins writes, "All is seared with trade; bleared, smeared with toil."

Witnesses from the Battle

Father Benigno Beltran is the priest from Smokey Mountain. Smokey Mountain is the name of a vast landfill in the Philippines, outside Manila, where 25,000 people lived amongst the trash. In his book *Faith and Struggle on Smokey Mountain*, Father Beltran tells how he went to live with the poorest of the poor, who scavenged among the stinking, smoking landfill for whatever they were able to salvage, recycle, and resell.

In our greedy, consumerist culture, we do not simply pollute and destroy the natural world; we also pollute and destroy our greatest resource — our fellow human beings. When you see the pollution of the world in places like Smokey Mountain, you also see the pollution and destruction of human beings. When you see the faces of the children who were born and raised on Smokey Mountain and similar slums around the developing world, you see the innocence of God's children who were restored by Christ's resurrection but are still being soiled and despoiled by Satan and sin.

Father Beltran spent thirty years of his life working with the poor on Smokey Mountain. He helped them build a church, start a school, and form a cooperative. He worked with the authorities to provide health care, homes, and a way to eventually close and redevelop the site. Through his efforts, the light of Christ's resurrection was shining through his Body, the Church.

Meditate for Victory

Can you see the sunrise and feel the cool breeze as Mary Magdalene hurries to the garden to finish burying the one she loved? Everything about the spring morning speaks of new life, new innocence, and a new beginning. Older traditions held that Mary Magdalene was a prostitute, but the Gospels simply say that she was the woman who was delivered from the oppression of seven demons.

What is clear is that Mary's fallen condition was a picture of our polluted, soiled, Satan-dominated world. Mary Magdalene was set free and given a fresh start by Jesus. Her innocence was restored. She was a girl again. His healing and redeeming love brought her to her own inner resurrection. That which was old was made new. That which was polluted, dead, and dying was restored completely on that Easter morning.

As you meditate on this bright promise, see how the Lord has healed you and given you a fresh start. Turn again with your prayer to be restored and renewed in Christ. Ask that the fresh life of the Resurrection might surge through you and that the power of Christ might banish the greed, lust, corruption, and pollution in the world, and restore again our humanity's innocence.

Battle Points

On each bead, pray to support one of these good intentions:

- For children whose lives are corrupted by lust and greed
- For those who work to protect the innocent
- For the poorest of the poor
- For those who strive for economic justice for the poor
- For those whose lives are ruined by the pollution of sin and despair
- For those who work with the poor in the developing world
- For victims of environmental disaster and those who help them
- For those who work for environmental cleanup and protection

- For those who work to establish humane treatment of animals
- For those who work to clean up political and economic corruption

_____

After the Fátima Prayer

Heavenly Father, you created the world in great
love and restored your creation with an even greater
love. Look with mercy on your broken and wounded
creation. Restore the innocence, truth, and beauty of
your lost children. Help those who strive to restore
your soiled world, and strengthen those who strive for
economic justice and peace for the poor.
All of this we ask in the name of the
resurrected Lord Jesus Christ. Amen.

_____

Ascension

Souls in Purgatory

(Luke 24:50-51)

After his resurrection, Jesus' mission is finished, and he has to return to his Father in heaven. He gathers his disciples together, teaching them and showing them more of the Father's plan. After giving them final instructions to go into all the world to preach the Gospel, he is received into heavenly glory. His ascension into heaven is the final step of freedom. His earthly pilgrimage is over, and he is heading home at last. The Ascension is the final stage of the journey. The work is done. Mission accomplished. Welcome home.

The Dark Distortion

Where Jesus goes, we are destined to go. He came to this earth to rescue the lost sons and daughters of Eve and bring us home. To reach heaven is our destiny and our final freedom. For this, Christ redeemed us. For this, we were baptized. For this, we walked by faith through this valley of tears. Heaven is our home country, death is the return of the prodigal son from exile, and reaching the glory is our ultimate destiny.

Satan will do everything he can to keep us from completing that journey and going home with Christ the Savior. He distorts our vision and tries to keep our focus on this earthly world and its concerns. He tries to distract us from our true goal and our final destiny. He tempts us away from the call to grow up into the full humanity of Christ Jesus (Eph 3:18).

He keeps us earthbound so that we will not ascend to heaven with Christ, and he tempts us to mortal sin so that, if possible, we will spend eternity in hell. If he can't achieve our damnation, he wants us to be weighed down with attachments to our sin through lust, greed, and selfishness. He does not want us to continue on our path of purification in this life.

If we do not continue on our path of purification, which leads finally to heaven with Christ, we will have to be purified in purgatory after this earthly life is over. Purgatory is not the devil's final victory because all the souls in purgatory will eventually complete their purification and be with Christ in glory. Nevertheless, purgatory represents time wasted on earth and a minor victory for Satan in his ongoing war against heaven.

Witnesses from the Battle

C. Bernard Ruffin, in his book *Padre Pio: The True Story*, shares the following episode in the life of the saint. One winter afternoon, after a heavy snowfall, Padre Pio was sitting by the fireplace in the friary's guest room. While he was immersed in prayer, an old man, wearing an old-fashioned cloak that was, at the time, still favored by southern Italian peasants, sat down beside him. Concerning this man, Padre Pio later stated: "I could not imagine how he could have entered the friary at this time of night [since all the doors were locked]. I questioned him: 'Who are you? What do you want?'"

The old man replied, "Padre Pio, I am Pietro Di Mauro, son of Nicola, nicknamed Precoco." He then continued: "I died in this friary on the 18th of September, 1908, in cell number 4, when it was still [a poorhouse]. One night, while in bed, I fell asleep with a lighted cigar, which ignited the [mattress] and I died, suffocated and burned. I am still in purgatory. I need a holy Mass in order to be freed. God permitted that I come and ask you for help."

After offering Mass for the poor soul, Padre Pio went to the local records office and confirmed the details of the friar's tragic death.

Purgatory is more like a reform school than a prison. It is a place where purification is completed, and the beautiful truth about purgatory is that our prayers can help the souls who are being purified there.

Father F. X. Schouppe's book *Purgatory: Explained by the Lives and Legends of the Saints* outlines how powerful it is for Masses to be said for the repose of the souls in purgatory. After the Mass, it is the Rosary, combined with sufferings and sacrifices here on this earth, that most helps to win the battles of purgatory for the poor souls.

Meditate for Victory

The disciples watched as Jesus was taken up into heaven from them. Can you sense their wonder and amazement? After he had gone, the angels told them to get busy, for there was still work to be done.

This is the truth of the Ascension for us. As we meditate on this mystery, we see Jesus taken up from us, but we also see the work that remains. The work is first for ourselves, that we will renew our commitment to live the resurrection life while we still have time here on this earth. Now is the day of salvation, and now is the day for continuing our work of purification, because it is easier to accomplish this task here in the physical realm than it is after death.

It is the power of Jesus' resurrection and ascension that gives us the power on earth to complete this work. The power by which he rose from the dead and ascended to heaven is at work in us through the Holy Spirit. To conclude the meditation, focus on the work of purification you have to do, the souls in purgatory you might pray for, and the realization that you do this in the power of the Holy Spirit, who is the focus of the next Glorious mystery.

Battle Points

On each bead, pray to support one of these good intentions:

- For those who are near death
- For those who are dying separated from God's love
- That we might not die unprepared
- For priests who minister the sacraments to the dying
- For doctors and nurses who minister in hospices for the dying
- For those who are bereaved
- For the eternal rest of the souls of our loved ones
- For the souls of our ancestors
- For the eternal rest of the souls of priests and religious
- For the eternal rest of the souls who have been forgotten

After the Fátima Prayer

Heavenly Father, your Son, Jesus Christ, died,
rose again and ascended into glory so that the way
to heaven might be opened to all who believe.
Strengthen and encourage those who have died in
Christ's love. Send your holy angels to assist them as
they continue their journey to purification and final
glory. Help us always to be aware of your great love
and to use aright the time that is left to us here on
earth. Amen.

Pentecost

Ideologies of Deception and Theft

(Acts 2:2-4)

Eleven timid men waited for the gift that had been prom-
ised, with the mother of Jesus in their midst. Then the super-
natural gift of the Holy Spirit was poured out. There was a
rushing wind, and tongues "as of fire" hovered over each of
them. When they spoke, even foreign visitors to Jerusalem
understood their words, which totally amazed their listen-
ers. Suddenly, their natural gifts were amplified by God's
power, and the Church was born. The Spirit-filled Church
is a sign to the world of a different order of creation. The
Church is the Body of Christ alive in the world today. It
is an international brotherhood of men and women united
across all nationalities, ethnicities, races, and cultures. The
Spirit-filled Church strives to be a community of peace and
justice for all.

The Dark Distortion

In the creation of the Church, God intended a new kind of
human family to be born. Men were called to humbly love
their wives and sacrifice themselves as Christ loved the Church
(Eph 5:25). Women were called to live in humble service to
their families. Children were called to obey their parents in
loving service. The family example was extended to the Church,

and from the Church to the world. In the power of the Holy Spirit, human society was meant to grow into a harmonious, loving family of mutual service for the common good.

Such a utopia is despised by Satan. The last thing he wants is for human beings to live together in simplicity, love, and mutual service for the common good. Instead, he twists this Spirit-filled ideal with ideologies that counterfeit the common good. Instead of mutual self-sacrifice, he sells people the idea of the self-service of "free markets" where (with a lack of virtue) greed is rewarded and selfishness idealized. On the other side of the battlefield, he is also busy selling people a counterfeit idea of community through communism, through which a government uses force to create false equality.

Both ideologies are rooted in self-service and theft. Selfishness and theft destroy trust — and when trust is destroyed, the family, the community, and the nation are destroyed. Instead of a Spirit-filled family of people and nations, Satan has created a spite-filled collection of warring parties, warring ideologies, and warring nations.

The Spirit brings sharing, liberty, unity, and solidarity. Satan brings selfishness, slavery, division, and strife.

Witnesses from the Battle

Every Easter week, our family used to attend a Catholic charismatic festival called "Celebrate." Teaching sessions were streamed for different age groups, Eucharistic Adoration was available 24/7, and the main hall hosted large-scale worship sessions, with dynamic speakers from around the country.

At its best, the charismatic movement focused on the unity, joy, and peace that come from being filled with the Holy Spirit. We were one family in the Spirit, and as one family we were able to accomplish not just a joyful atmosphere of praise and worship but also a genuine growth in God.

The unity, joy, and peace of the Holy Spirit are present in every community truly driven by faith in Christ. The Spirit's presence overflows into genuine love and concern for others. Where the Spirit of the Lord is, the poor are accepted and assisted, the sick and the dying are loved, the young are nurtured, and the elderly and lonely are cared for.

Such Spirit-filled communities challenge and subvert the ideologies of the world that are based on self-serving greed, theft, and the lust for power.

Meditate for Victory

The Spirit came on the apostles and the Blessed Mother in tongues of flame and the sound of a mighty rushing wind. Can you imagine this? It is God's firestorm and hurricane to turn the world and its ideologies upside down.

As you meditate, think how much your own life is dominated by the concerns of the world. Think how much time you spend worrying about money, discussing politics, and debating the methods of worldly power. Isn't it a waste of your time? What if your life were totally swept away by the firestorm and tempest of God's Holy Spirit?

Imagine that fire and that wind transforming your life, and pray for those who are caught up in the false ideologies, hopes, and dreams of this world. Pray for their conversion, and imagine the fire of God's love burning up Satan's false dreams and the mighty wind of God's new creation sweeping through your family, your community, and our world.

Can praying the Rosary really change the course of human events? Of course it can, because praying the Rosary changes the person who prays it. If all people prayed the Rosary, they would draw closer to God, serve others in humility, and help naturally to build up all that makes for peace and the common good.

Battle Points

On each bead, pray to support one of these good intentions:

- To be filled with the Holy Spirit
- For our families to be filled with the Holy Spirit
- For our parishes and priests to be filled with the Holy Spirit
- For our dioceses and bishops to be filled with the Holy Spirit
- For the spirit of generosity and charity to prevail
- For those who are dominated by envy and tempted to steal
- To be delivered from the spirit of greed and lust for power
- For those ensnared by the dreams of political and economic utopias
- For politicians to work for the common good
- For diplomats to seek peace, justice, and the common good

After the Fátima Prayer

Lord God, you sent the Holy Spirit among us for the perfection of your people and the establishment of your Church on earth. Deliver us from worldly dreams and ambitions, and help us seek the true brotherhood of the Body of Christ. Give us the spirit of freedom, love, and charity for all so that by your Holy Spirit we may serve the common good and build up your community of love in the world. Amen.

Assumption

Materialism

(Ephesians 2:4-7)

The most remarkable thing about the life of the Blessed Virgin is that because of the mystery of the Incarnation, a new relationship was established between the physical and the spiritual realm. God was no longer just "out there," cut off from the physical realm. He was also "in here," taking human flesh and being part of human history. After the Resurrection and Pentecost, Mary passed the rest of her earthly life in the background. Tradition tells us she lived with the apostle John until the time came for her to leave her earthly life. We aren't sure how it happened, nor do we know with certainty who was there at the time, but the simplest version of the story is that Mary was surrounded by the apostles when she died, or "fell asleep." Afterward, her body was not in the tomb, and the Church realized that, just as she shared in her son's life and death in an intimate way, she must also have shared in his resurrection in a unique way. His participation in her physical life brought about her participation in his heavenly life. Because she shared in his sorrows, she also shared in his ultimate and total victory.

The Dark Distortion

Through the mystery of the Incarnation, a new relationship between heaven and earth is established and a new potential for every human being is made possible. By sharing in Christ's life completely, the Virgin Mary shows us what is possible. We are able, as St. Paul says, to grow up into the full humanity of Christ Jesus (Eph 4:13), and in his letter to the Romans, chapter 5, he says that we might become the righteousness of God in Christ. The path each one of us has through life is to become all that God created us to be. We are to become saints — ordinary people who have been transformed by the extraordinary grace of God to become Christians — "little Christs." This destiny of glory is seen perfectly in the final work of grace in Mary's life: her assumption into heaven.

Satan, however, wants to destroy this destiny. He hates the idea that we might grow ever closer to Christ and finally attain the full humanity to which we are called. He will do everything he can to keep us locked in the appetites and desires of this physical world. Through gluttony, drunkenness, lust, and greed, he enslaves us, making us dependent and holding back the progress of our souls. He keeps us chained to the material realm and keeps our eyes distracted from the beauty and hope of heaven.

We are called to love the good things that God has created, but not to love them more than him. Our relationship with material possessions and pleasures is one in which we love all things according to their worth … but no more. As St. Benedict teaches, we are to "prefer nothing to the love of Christ." Satan, however, wants us to fix our eyes only on the things we can see and to forget the spiritual realities.

To keep us locked in this material world, Satan propagates a whole range of false philosophies. Materialism is the idea that there is no supernatural realm. Utilitarianism is the philosophy that teaches that the only virtue is what is practical and cost-effective in this physical realm. Scientism is the idea that the only valid knowledge is scientific knowledge. These philosophies keep our eyes down and lead us to deny the heavenly realities.

Witnesses from the Battle

Jeanine didn't seem like a wicked person. She was polite and pleasant enough, but when I got to know her I realized there was a part of her that was missing. It was as if she were not fully human.

Jeanine was very absorbed in her appearance. She spent thousands of dollars on clothes, cosmetic surgery, makeup, and hair. She had an addition built onto her home to house the extra closet space she needed for all her clothes and shoes. She spent even more money on her nice cars, her trophy lake house, and dressing her husband and her two "perfect" children.

Jeanine was not just suffering from a mild case of "shop until you drop"; she was totally consumed by her materialism. Envy had eaten her up, and her shopping had become her drug. Not only that, her addiction to material things blocked her spiritual life. The only reason she went to church was so that she might look good to others.

Jeanine finally had a breakdown when her husband had an affair and told her the main reason he didn't love her anymore was because she was shallow and selfish. That was his way of saying that she had no depth to her life or her personality.

When she began to take her spiritual life seriously, Jeanine found a deeper side to her life. God healed wounds from the past, and through praying the Rosary she learned to connect with the eternal soul that God had created within her but which had been lying dormant. She never got her husband back, but her perspective changed and she began to realize that true joy could be found only in loving God and others.

Meditate for Victory

Mary's assumption into heaven was the final victory of God's grace in her life. Her identification with her son was complete. His grace gathering her up into his presence was a picture of the final sharing in his glory that all of us are called to, in our own way and through our own path of providence. Her assumption was a fulfillment of the earthly and heavenly in one great transaction.

As you meditate on what God did for the Blessed Virgin Mary, imagine what great things he wants to do for you. He knows how you are made. He knew you before you were in your mother's womb, and he knows what greatness he has in store for you. He wants the eternal part of you to come alive so that you might be transformed from glory to glory.

Visualize Mary's assumption into complete glory as a sign also of the transformation of the whole human race and of the whole of God's creation. St. Paul says that the whole creation "has been groaning with labor pains" (Rom 8:22) for the redemption and completion in glory that God has in store. Then see the sad distortion of this glory that we share in. See the twisted, sad decline of our race into envy, vanity, and pathetic self-absorption. Then envision instead the transformation of the physical realm from the inside out as all that we are becomes infused with the supernatural graces from above.

Battle Points

On each bead, pray to support one of these good intentions:

- For all who strive to be completely fulfilled in Christ
- For those who are locked in the sin of envy

- For those whose lives have no spiritual dimension
- For those whose lives are consumed with worldly ambition
- For those who care for nothing but efficiency and money
- For those who are obsessed by vanity and their reputation
- For those who are addicted to material possessions
- For atheists and those who deny the supernatural realm
- For guidance and protection of the guardian angels
- For deliverance from lies and distortions of the truth by Satan

---

After the Fátima Prayer

Lord God, in the Blessed Virgin Mary you reveal to
humanity our true goal, our destiny, and our home.
Deliver us from all vanity and pride in our ambitions.
Teach us to follow in the path of Mary, who was
assumed into heaven because she was the most
humble person on earth. Finally, bring us and your
whole human family to that final supernatural glory
which you have prepared for us, world without end.
Amen.

Coronation

Corruption and Condemnation of Humanity

(Revelation 12:1-2)

The Coronation of the Blessed Virgin as Queen of heaven is an event beyond our imagining. Needless to say, we don't have an eyewitness to her ultimate glorification, but the Book of Revelation gives us the next best thing. The apostle John has visions of heaven and the end of all things. In one of the visions, recorded in the twelfth chapter, John sees a woman "clothed with the sun, with the moon under her feet, and on her head a crown of twelve stars" (Rev 12:1). This woman's son is the Messiah, the ruler over all, and this reveals the woman to be the Mother of the Messiah — Mary. From this vision of heaven, the Church has praised God for the final glory that Jesus shares with his mother — a share in his eternal kingdom as the Queen of heaven.

The Dark Distortion

The Blessed Virgin's coronation as Queen of heaven is a realization of the reality and beauty of our heavenly home. Heaven is the summary and gathering together of all that is beautiful, good, and true. The Virgin Mary — the most glorious of created beings — sums up in herself the completely redeemed creation and the epitome of all that is beautiful, good, and true. She sits at the right hand of her son so that in them we see the kingdom of heaven. We see all that is harmonious, all that is complete, perfect, humble, and whole. In them, we see everything as it should be — natural, simple, infinite, awesome, and "Yes!"

Satan's destiny is the opposite. His eternal home is hell, and hell is the summary of everything dark, distorted, and destroyed. Hell is a cacophony of noise, dissidence, dismay, and despair. In hell, everything good, beautiful, and true has been finally distorted into that which is evil, disfigured, and false. Hell is the great Gehenna prepared for Satan and his angels. Hell is real, and Satan wants to corrupt and condemn as many human souls as possible.

Hell is prepared for all souls who finally reject the mercy and love of God. Will human souls go to hell? We must admit that there are many in this life who turn with rage and hatred against all that is beautiful, good, and true, so we must conclude that many of them will continue to rage against God and reject all that is beautiful, good, and true.

Every day we have a choice to come closer to the great Mercy or to reject God's love. Every day we have a choice to pursue all that is beautiful, good, and true, or to cling to those corrupt loves that are distorted, evil, and false. We can follow heaven and receive our crowns of glory with Mary, or we can follow the dark angels and receive the condemnation of eternal torment and separation from God.

Witnesses from the Battle

I was called to the hospital late one night to anoint a man who was dying. Richard had been a Catholic his whole life. A regular at daily Mass, he worked with the poor in the food pantry, sang in the choir, and loved his local parish. His quiet life of prayer and service was an example to all he met. After his wife died, his faith deepened, and as his own health failed he became increasingly a man of prayer and contemplation.

Richard was lying in the hospital bed with his daughter and grandchildren by his side. The doctors had done all they could for him. So I asked the family to step outside while I heard Richard's confession. When they returned, we prayed together, I anointed him, and we prayed the prayers of passing. Then I could see Richard was trying to speak to me.

I leaned forward. He whispered something to me, but I couldn't make it out. We looked into his eyes. They were suddenly glowing with a new fervor as he gazed beyond us to the corner of the room. I leaned over again to hear what he had to say. This time I could understand him.

He smiled a huge smile and said, "It's Christ the King!" Then he closed his eyes. He was at peace, and he passed away later that night.

Another time, I went to anoint a woman who was dying. She had been restless and afraid. After the prayers, she was at peace. A few months later I met the caregiver who had been there. She was a Baptist Christian, and she said: "That was the most beautiful thing I have ever seen. Praise God! I want that when I die!"

I have experienced many such passings. The witness to those living is always powerful and moving, and it is always a reminder that heaven is waiting for those who love God and who are called according to his purpose.

Meditate for Victory

The Coronation of the Blessed Virgin is, in a way, the crowning of the whole Church. All of the redeemed will share at last in the crown of glory that God gives to his adopted sons and daughters — for if we are adopted children of the King, that makes each one of us a prince and princess in the kingdom. As you meditate on this mystery, meditate on the glory of heaven that awaits you. Your destiny is to take your place in heaven. Once your purification is complete, you, too, will share in the glory that is prepared for all of God's children. That glory is the final sharing in all that is beautiful, eternal, good, and true.

Meditate also on the glory that will be when the whole of creation is redeemed. God will gather up all things and bring them into his eternal purpose. Nothing will be wasted. All will be harvest. All will be harmony. All will be peace. Then we will see that even the bad things we did will be turned to our glory, for they will have brought us one step closer to home.

Battle Points

On each bead, pray to support one of these good intentions:

- For all who wage spiritual warfare against the powers of darkness
- For all who are cooperating with God's grace on their path to heaven
- For the intercession of our patron saints
- For the intercession of the holy angels
- For those who preach to souls in rebellion against God
- For those who rebel in pride against the beauty, truth, and goodness of God
- For atheists and agnostics who do not believe in hell

- For those who delight in their sin and rebel against the kingdom of heaven
- For those who choose hell over heaven in this life
- For those who worship Satan and his angels

_____

After the Fátima Prayer

Heavenly Father, your Son, Jesus Christ, has gone before us to prepare a place for us in heaven. Open our hearts to the wonders of his love, and help us always to seek that which is beautiful, good, and true. Draw all your children to your love, and deliver them from the bondage of Satan and from those angels that would drag them down to hell forever. Save them from their slavery to sin, and bring them at last to your heavenly home, with the Blessed Virgin Mary and all the angels and saints. Amen.

_____

CONCLUSION

One of the benefits of praying the Rosary for spiritual warfare is that we cooperate with God to fight against evil in the world. This changes the world, but it also changes us. As we pray to strengthen the positive activities in the world, our perspective changes. We begin to see all the good things God is doing, and all the good works his people are engaged in. Praying the Rosary for spiritual warfare turns our fear into hope and our anger into joy. God is good, and we can see that the darkness can never overwhelm the light.

We fight against the spiritual forces of wickedness in high places, but we fight with joy in our soul, and with the surge of hope in our hearts. Because of the resurrection of Jesus Christ, we are happy warriors, a band of brothers and sisters who cannot be overcome. This does not mean the battle is easy and that we do not face the most terrible tribulations, but in all these things we know that because Christ has won the victory we will share the victory.

This optimism runs through the New Testament like a golden thread. Despite persecution, imprisonment, misunderstanding, and conflict, St. Paul retains his joy. In the beautiful King James Version of the Bible we read his words:

> What shall we then say to these things? If God be for us, who can be against us? He that spared not his own Son, but delivered him up for us all, how shall he not with him also freely give us all things? Who shall lay any thing to the charge of God's elect? It is God that

justifieth. Who is he that condemneth? It is Christ that died, yea rather, that is risen again, who is even at the right hand of God, who also maketh intercession for us. Who shall separate us from the love of Christ? shall tribulation, or distress, or persecution, or famine, or nakedness, or peril, or sword? As it is written, For thy sake we are killed all the day long; we are accounted as sheep for the slaughter. Nay, in all these things we are more than conquerors through him that loved us. For I am persuaded, that neither death, nor life, nor angels, nor principalities, nor powers, nor things present, nor things to come, Nor height, nor depth, nor any other creature, shall be able to separate us from the love of God, which is in Christ Jesus our Lord. (Rom 8:31-39)

Therefore I encourage you to pray the Rosary for spiritual warfare not with fear, anger, or bitterness in your heart, but always and everywhere with the same abundant joy that the Blessed Virgin experienced.

In Mary, we see what great things God has done:

"He has shown strength with his arm,
he has scattered the proud in the imagination of their
    hearts,
he has put down the mighty from their thrones,
and exalted those of low degree;
he has filled the hungry with good things,
and the rich he has sent empty away." (Lk 1:51-53)

In her, we see these truths lived out. In her, the battle is accomplished, for she is the forerunner of what God will accomplish in the whole of humanity. The battle may be bleak and the war long, but with Jesus and Mary there is always the glimpse of dawn in the darkness and the echo of a victory song.

APPENDIX A
Prayers of the Rosary

Sign of the Cross

In the name of the Father, and of the Son, and of the Holy Spirit. Amen.

Apostles' Creed

I believe in God, the Father almighty, creator of heaven and earth; and in Jesus Christ, his only Son, our Lord; who was conceived by the Holy Spirit, born of the Virgin Mary, suffered under Pontius Pilate, was crucified, died, and was buried. He descended to the dead; the third day he arose again from the dead. He ascended into heaven and sits at the right hand of God, the Father almighty; from thence he shall come to judge the living and the dead. I believe in the Holy Spirit, the holy catholic Church, the communion of saints, the forgiveness of sins, the resurrection of the body, and life everlasting. Amen.

Our Father

Our Father, who art in heaven, hallowed be thy name. Thy kingdom come. Thy will be done on earth, as it is in heaven. Give us this day our daily bread, and forgive us our trespasses, as we forgive those who trespass against us, and lead us not into temptation, but deliver us from evil. Amen.

Hail Mary

Hail Mary, full of grace. The Lord is with thee. Blessed art thou among women, and blessed is the fruit of thy womb, Jesus. Holy Mary, Mother of God, pray for us sinners, now and at the hour of our death. Amen.

Glory Be

Glory be to the Father, and to the Son, and to the Holy Spirit. As it was in the beginning, is now, and ever shall be, world without end. Amen.

Fátima Prayer

O my Jesus, forgive us our sins, save us from the fires of hell, lead all souls to heaven, especially those who have most need of your mercy. Amen.

Hail, Holy Queen

Hail, holy Queen, Mother of Mercy, our life, our sweetness, and our hope. To thee do we cry, poor banished children of Eve; to thee do we send up our sighs, mourning, and weeping in this valley of tears. Turn then, most gracious advocate, thine eyes of mercy toward us, and after this, our exile, show unto us the blessed fruit of thy womb, Jesus. O clement, O loving, O sweet Virgin Mary.

V. Pray for us, O Holy Mother of God.

R. That we may be made worthy of the promises of Christ.

Hail, Holy Queen (Latin)

Salve, Regina, Mater misericordiæ,
vita, dulcedo, et spes nostra, salve.
Ad te clamamus exsules filii Hevæ.
Ad te suspiramus, gementes et flentes
in hac lacrimarum valle.
Eia, ergo, advocata nostra, illos tuos
misericordes oculos ad nos converte.
Et Iesum, benedictum fructum ventris tui,
nobis post hoc exsilium ostende.
O clemens, O pia, O dulcis Virgo Maria.

V. Ora pro nobis, sancta Dei Genitrix.

R. Ut digni efficiamur promissionibus Christi.

Concluding Rosary Prayer

Let us pray: O God, whose only-begotten Son, by his life, death, and resurrection, has purchased for us the rewards of eternal life, grant, we beseech thee, that meditating upon these mysteries of the Most Holy Rosary of the Blessed Virgin Mary, we may imitate what they contain and obtain what they promise, through the same Christ our Lord. Amen.

Prayer to St. Michael the Archangel

St. Michael the Archangel, defend us in battle. Be our defense against the wickedness and snares of the devil. May God rebuke him, we humbly pray. And do you, O prince of the heavenly hosts, by the power of God, thrust into hell Satan and all the evil spirits, who prowl about the world seeking the ruin of souls. Amen.

APPENDIX B

Praying the Lord's Prayer for Spiritual Warfare

I once attended a seminar on the deliverance ministry, conducted by the author and psychiatrist Kenneth McCall. During the questions and answers, three rather excitable women told Dr. McCall that there was a witches' coven meeting in their town, and they wondered how to get rid of it.

Dr. McCall was a very soft-spoken man with a deep spirituality. He said quietly, "In my experience, in most cases, all that is necessary to rid a place of evil is for a small group of committed Christians to gather and pray silently together and then repeat the Lord's Prayer together, concentrating on the phrase 'Deliver us from evil.'" He smiled and then added, "That usually works. Any further questions?"

I think the ladies were a bit disappointed. Perhaps they wanted a dramatic exorcism, complete with spinning heads, levitations, holy water, and amazing signs and wonders.

I have remembered Dr. McCall's answer and use the Lord's Prayer as a weapon against evil. I also teach others to do the same.

Sometimes an exorcism is needed, in which case only a trained exorcist may perform the rite with the bishop's permission.

However, all baptized Christians are called to be soldiers in the spiritual battle, and a conscious use of the Lord's Prayer for deliverance is a practical, down-to-earth way to defeat evil. We sometimes forget that a major dimension of the Lord's ministry was his battle with Satan. From the moment of his baptism, Jesus is thrust out into the desert to confront the father of lies. Immediately, we see him casting out demons; healing the sick, in body, mind, or spirit; and finally, through his cross and resurrection, he tramples the ancient foe once and for all.

He has given us the Our Father as a weapon in the war.

There are three phrases on which to concentrate. The first is "Forgive us our trespasses." We begin by asking for forgiveness of our sins, and this is linked with our action of forgiveness directed toward others. When we say the words "as we forgive those who trespass against us," we become conductors for God's forgiveness, which flows through us to others. In this double phrase, we accept forgiveness and so become channels of God's forgiveness. This is the important first step, and praying the Lord's Prayer this first time slowly brings a focus on that phrase. When this is combined with a good examination of conscience, our sins are forgiven, and we become the vessels for forgiveness so that God can work through us.

In this way, the Lord's Prayer becomes a sincere act of contrition. It should go without saying that if we are aware of mortal sin in our lives, then this act of contrition, which is built into the Lord's Prayer, should be supplemented with the Sacrament of Reconciliation.

How does the rest of the Lord's Prayer work as a weapon of spiritual warfare?

Praying the Lord's Prayer the second time, we focus on the phrase "Lead us not into temptation." This phrase is confusing to many people. Why would God lead us into temptation anyway? The problem is with the archaic language we use from a more traditional liturgy. "Lead us not into temptation" can also be translated as "Lead us away from temptation." By "tempting" we do not simply mean the attraction we feel toward sin, but instead we are referring to the active temptation that Satan puts before us. In other words, "Lord, defend us from the attack of the evil one" or "Keep us safe from the continued lure of evil. Direct us into the light and away from the dark."

This second time praying the Lord's Prayer is linked clearly with the third. The third time we pray, we focus on the phrase "Deliver us from evil." This is the final and most powerful prayer of deliverance. Deliverance ministry is just that: a liberation from bondage to evil.

It is too simplistic to imagine that bondage to Satan is only ever in the form of explicit demonic possession. Many people suffer from bondage to evil. Some are bound to addictions, obsessive sexual behaviors, or addictions to particular sins. Others are in bondage to toxic, evil relationships. Still others are in bondage to their negative self-esteem, destructive habits, depression, or fear and anxiety. In all of these difficulties, there can be a spiritual dimension. Evil spirits can hold us back from fullness of health and spiritual well-being.

In a very quiet and down-to-earth way, therefore, we can battle evil through a conscious and intentional use of the Lord's Prayer to receive and give forgiveness, to pray for freedom from temptation, and for deliverance from the dark powers that bind us.

Finally, the Lord's Prayer can be used in this way not only for ourselves but also as an intercession for others. It is an act of mercy to pray for others who are in bondage and to ask the Lord to set them free.

This prayer unites us with the prayer of Jesus. This is how he prayed. This is what he prayed for. I believe this aspect of the

Lord's Prayer is the most important and yet most neglected. When this prayer is said simply, quietly, and slowly, we join our prayers with his, and so join our will with his, for the salvation of the world and the liberation of souls.

APPENDIX C

Praying the Hail Mary for Spiritual Warfare

One of my favorite Catholic images is that of the Blessed Virgin Mary holding the child Jesus, standing on the globe and crowned with twelve stars, trampling a serpent under her feet, and offering the Rosary to the world.

This image, based on the twelfth chapter of the Book of Revelation, captures the majesty and power of the Virgin and her son. It captures the role they play in the battle against the ancient foe, the dragon.

Mary is a great warrior in the ongoing battle, and the Hail Mary, when broken down into separate phrases, can be a great meditation on, and identification with, the battles that Mary fights with us and for us.

When we say, "Hail Mary, full of grace," we acknowledge that her Immaculate Conception was powered and initiated by a full outpouring of God's grace into her life at the moment of her conception. This fullness of grace is what helps to defeat evil in the world. It is as if the desert of evil is flooded with the water of God's grace. It is as if the darkness of the night is filled with the glorious light of morning. It is Mary's grace-fullness that overwhelms evil as a tidal wave of God's goodness and mercy.

When we say, "The Lord is with thee," we are reminded that the battle against evil is never fought relying on our own strength but only as we put on "the whole armor of God" (Eph

6:11). It is only when the Lord is by our side that we can hope to participate in this battle.

The next phrase, "Blessed art thou among women, and blessed is the fruit of thy womb, Jesus," reminds us that the Hail Mary is a Christ-centered prayer. At the heart of the prayer is the powerful and blessed name of Jesus. The name of Jesus is like a pivot for the whole prayer. It is the "quiet focus" in the middle of the prayer. It is the point at which we focus on Jesus as the one who defeated Satan once and for all by his cross and resurrection. We sing "At the Name of Jesus Every Knee Shall Bow," and St. Paul teaches that at the name of Jesus every knee in heaven and on earth will bend (Phil 2:10). This name of Jesus, at the heart of the Hail Mary, is the name by which demons flee and Satan is vanquished.

Next, we say, "Holy Mary, Mother of God," and as we do so we are reminded that Mary is the Mother of God — not because God Almighty has a mother, but because Jesus is God Almighty in human flesh in human history. It is by the incarnation of the Son of God, who took flesh of the Immaculate Virgin, that we are redeemed, and that the evil in our lives and in the world is conquered.

Then we recite, "Pray for us sinners, now and at the hour of our death." Death is not just our physical death. It is possible that the soul can die through mortal sin, and so we ask our Mother to pray for us not only at the hour of our physical death but also as we face every aspect of death. The wages of sin is death. Satan and his demons bring death wherever they go. They love to kill, maim, distort, and destroy. Therefore, as we ask for Mary's prayers "at the hour of our death," we invoke her prayers to help us overcome every type of death through the power of her son's glorious resurrection.

Finally, we say, "Amen." Which is to say, "So Be It!"

APPENDIX D

Other Resources for Spiritual Warfare

The Warrior's Rosary: These beautiful rosaries are especially designed for spiritual warfare. The rosary beads are interspersed with medals of "warrior saints": http://www.the warriorsrosary.com/store/c1/Featured_Products.html.

Manual for Spiritual Warfare: This beautiful book, compiled by Paul Thigpen, gathers prayers and devotions for use in spiritual warfare: https://www.tanbooks.com/index.php/manual -for-spirtual-warfare.html.

Saints Who Battled Satan: Paul Thigpen gathers the stories of saints who battled Satan: https://www.tanbooks.com/index .php/saints-who-battled-satan-seventeen-holy-warriors-who -can-teach-you-how-to-fight-the-good-fight-and-vanquish -ancient-your-enemy.html.

Catholic Warriors: Visit this website for a wide selection of prayers, books, and devotions to help with spiritual warfare: https://www.catholicwarriors.com.

Praying the Rosary for Inner Healing: My first book on the Rosary will help bring the healing power of Christ into your memories and the depth of your own experience: http://dwight longenecker.com/shop/praying-the-rosary-for-inner-healing/.

The Screwtape Letters: In C. S. Lewis' classic book, a senior devil named Screwtape instructs a younger demon on how to tempt his human ward. This humorous but serious book will remind you how the devil works.

The Gargoyle Code and ***Slubgrip Instructs***: My own two books take C. S. Lewis' idea and bring it up to date for Catholics. In the first book, the demon Slubgrip writes e-mails to Dogwart, telling him how to tempt his Catholic patient. In the second book, Slubgrip is demoted to teach Popular Culture 101 in Bowelbages University in hell. Both books are structured to be read any time, but especially during Lent: http://dwightlonge necker.com/shop.

ABOUT THE AUTHOR

Dwight Longenecker is a former evangelical who became a priest in the Church of England before he and his family were received into full communion with the Catholic Church. He returned to his native United States and was ordained as a Catholic priest under the special pastoral provision for married former Anglican clergy.

Father Dwight is an award-winning blogger, author, and nationally known speaker. He contributes regularly to numerous papers, websites, and journals around the world, and he is a frequent guest on Catholic radio, EWTN, and nationwide news services.

He now serves as the parish priest of Our Lady of the Rosary Catholic Church in Greenville, South Carolina.

To browse his books, read his blog, and be in touch with Father Longenecker, visit dwightlongenecker.com.

Also by Dwight Longenecker

Praying the Rosary for Inner Healing

Discover the parallels between your life and the Mysteries of the Rosary while experiencing the healing graces of Our Lady. Where our lives are characterized by trauma, stress, pain, or sadness, this ancient contemplative prayer can bring acceptance, understanding, and joy.

Through a series of stories, reflections, and prayerful meditations, Fr. Longenecker reveals a powerful and very personal approach to using the Rosary as a process of transformation and healing from the inside out.

Available in hardback or digital version.

ID# T559

Fr. Dwight Longenecker's other books cover a wide range of Catholic topics from apologetics and theology to Benedictine spirituality and fiction.

Listen My Son: St. Benedict for Fathers is a book of daily readings that help apply the timeless wisdom of St. Benedict to family life. *St. Benedict and St. Thérèse — The Little Rule and the Little Way* is a study of the lives and writings of two of the most beloved saints. This book explores the simple, balanced spirituality of Benedict of Nursia and Thérèse of Lisieux.

More Christianity is the book Fr. Longenecker has written to explain the Catholic faith to evangelical Christians. Written in a friendly way, the book plays on the title of C. S. Lewis' famous *Mere Christianity* and shows how Catholicism is not something different, but something more. *Catholicism Pure and Simple* is a basic primer of Catholic catechesis. Beginning with arguments for God, it moves through to explain the role of Jesus and the Holy Spirit, the Church, prayer, and the sacraments.

C. S. Lewis' writings have had a huge impact, and Fr. Longenecker has borrowed Lewis' idea in *The Screwtape Letters* of an older demon writing to instruct a young student tempter. *The Gargoyle Code* and its sequel, *Slubgrip Instructs*, are both set out as Lent books. They take the reader on a descent into hell in order to rise up victorious.

Fr. Longenecker is also a popular speaker at retreats, men's conferences, parish missions, and on EWTN radio. You can follow his blog, browse his books, and be in touch at **dwightlongenecker.com**.